The Psalms Project Volume Six

Discovering the Spiritual World through the Psalms – Psalm 51-60

Michael Harvey Koplitz

All Scripture quotations, unless otherwise noted, are taken from the New American Standard Bible®, Copyright © 1960, 1962, 1963, 1968, 1971, 1972, 1973, 1975, 1977, 1995 by the Lockman Foundation. Used by permission (www.Lockman.org)

The NASB uses italic to indicate words that have been added for clarification. Citations are shown with large capital letters.

TABLE OF CONTENTS

The goal of this project:

This research project will examine the 150 psalms for the spiritual awareness each Psalm offers. Each Psalm will be examined by its language and the commentary of the Sages. The spiritual awareness analysis will be done in alignment with Ari's definition of the Tree of life, the Book of Creation, and the Zohar. Each verse of the Psalm will be rewritten using the intent of the language and spiritual commentary to convey its spiritual lesson.

The main resources:

The Zohar

The Book of Creation

Ari's writing on the Tree of Life and the Ten Sefirot

The Theological Wordbook of the Old Testament

Samson Hirsch's commentary on the Psalms

Tehillim – Psalms – A new translation with a commentary anthologized from the Talmudic and rabbinic sources

Accordance Bible Software

Psalm 51

New American Standard 1995	Hebrew

New American Standard 1995

Psa. 51:0 For the choir director. A Psalm of David, when [†]Nathan the prophet came to him, after he had gone in to Bathsheba.

Psa. 51:1   [a]Be gracious to me, O God, according to Your loving-kindness;
      According to the greatness of [b]Your compassion [c]blot out my transgressions.
2   [a]Wash me thoroughly from my iniquity
      And [b]cleanse me from my sin.
3   For [1]I [a]know my transgressions,
      And my sin is ever before me.
4   [a]Against You, You only, I have sinned
      And done what is [b]evil in Your sight,
      So that [c]You [1]are justified [2]when You speak
      And [3]blameless when You judge.

Psa. 51:5   Behold, I was [a]brought forth in iniquity,
      And in sin my mother conceived me.
6   Behold, You desire [a]truth in the [1]innermost being,
      And in the hidden part You will [b]make me know wisdom.
7   [1]Purify me [a]with hyssop, and I shall be clean;
      [2]Wash me, and I shall be [b]whiter than snow.

Hebrew

Psa. 51:1 לַמְנַצֵּחַ מִזְמוֹר
לְדָוִד ׃

Psa. 51:2 בְּבוֹא־אֵלָיו נָתָן
הַנָּבִיא כַּאֲשֶׁר־בָּא אֶל־בַּת־
שֶׁבַע ׃ 3 חָנֵּנִי אֱלֹהִים
כְּחַסְדֶּךָ כְּרֹב רַחֲמֶיךָ מְחֵה
פְשָׁעָי ׃ 4 הֶרֶב [הֶרֶב]
כַּבְּסֵנִי מֵעֲוֺנִי וּמֵחַטָּאתִי
טַהֲרֵנִי ׃ 5 כִּי־פְשָׁעַי אֲנִי
אֵדָע וְחַטָּאתִי נֶגְדִּי תָמִיד ׃ 6
לְךָ לְבַדְּךָ חָטָאתִי וְהָרַע
בְּעֵינֶיךָ עָשִׂיתִי לְמַעַן תִּצְדַּק
בְּדָבְרֶךָ תִּזְכֶּה בְשָׁפְטֶךָ ׃ 7
הֵן־בְּעָווֹן חוֹלָלְתִּי וּבְחֵטְא
יֶחֱמַתְנִי אִמִּי ׃ 8 הֵן־אֱמֶת
חָפַצְתָּ בַטֻּחוֹת וּבְסָתֻם
חָכְמָה תוֹדִיעֵנִי ׃ 9 תְּחַטְּאֵנִי
בְאֵזוֹב וְאֶטְהָר תְּכַבְּסֵנִי

8 ¹Make me to hear ᵃjoy and gladness,

Let the ᵇbones which You have broken rejoice.

9 ᵃHide Your face from my sins
And blot out all my iniquities.

Psa. 51:10 ᵃCreate ¹in me a ᵇclean heart, O God,

And renew ²a ᶜsteadfast spirit within me.

11 ᵃDo not cast me away from Your presence

And do not take Your ᵇHoly Spirit from me.

12 Restore to me the ᵃjoy of Your salvation

And sustain me with a ᵇwilling spirit.

13 *Then* I will ᵃteach transgressors Your ways,

And sinners will ¹be ᵇconverted to You.

Psa. 51:14 Deliver me from ᵃbloodguiltiness, O God, ᵇthe God of my salvation;

Then my ᶜtongue will joyfully sing of Your righteousness.

15 O Lord, ¹ᵃopen my lips,
That my mouth may ᵇdeclare Your praise.

16 For You ᵃdo not delight in sacrifice, otherwise I would give it;

You are not pleased with burnt offering.

17 The sacrifices of God are a ᵃbroken spirit;

A broken and a contrite heart, O God, You will not despise.

וּמִשֶּׁלֶג אַלְבִּין : 10 תַּשְׁמִיעֵנִי
שָׂשׂוֹן וְשִׂמְחָה תָּגֵלְנָה עֲצָמוֹת
דִּכִּיתָ : 11 הַסְתֵּר פָּנֶיךָ
מֵחֲטָאָי וְכָל־עֲוֺנֹתַי מְחֵה :
12 לֵב טָהוֹר בְּרָא־לִי
אֱלֹהִים וְרוּחַ נָכוֹן חַדֵּשׁ
בְּקִרְבִּי : 13 אַל־תַּשְׁלִיכֵנִי
מִלְּפָנֶיךָ וְרוּחַ קָדְשְׁךָ אַל־
תִּקַּח מִמֶּנִּי : 14 הָשִׁיבָה לִי
שְׂשׂוֹן יִשְׁעֶךָ וְרוּחַ נְדִיבָה
תִסְמְכֵנִי : 15 אֲלַמְּדָה
פֹשְׁעִים דְּרָכֶיךָ וְחַטָּאִים
אֵלֶיךָ יָשׁוּבוּ : 16 הַצִּילֵנִי
מִדָּמִים אֱלֹהִים אֱלֹהֵי
תְּשׁוּעָתִי תְּרַנֵּן לְשׁוֹנִי
צִדְקָתֶךָ : 17 אֲדֹנָי שְׂפָתַי
תִּפְתָּח וּפִי יַגִּיד תְּהִלָּתֶךָ : 18
כִּי לֹא־תַחְפֹּץ זֶבַח וְאֶתֵּנָה
עוֹלָה לֹא תִרְצֶה : 19 זִבְחֵי
אֱלֹהִים רוּחַ נִשְׁבָּרָה לֵב־
נִשְׁבָּר וְנִדְכֶּה אֱלֹהִים לֹא
תִבְזֶה : 20 הֵיטִיבָה בִרְצוֹנְךָ
אֶת־צִיּוֹן תִּבְנֶה חוֹמוֹת

Psa. 51:18   *a*By Your favor do good to Zion;

1*b*Build the walls of Jerusalem.

19   Then You will delight in 1*a*righteous sacrifices,

In *b*burnt offering and whole burnt offering;

Then 2young bulls will be offered on Your altar.

אֶז תַּחְפֹּץ **21** : יְרוּשָׁלָ‍ִם

אֶז וְכָלִיל עוֹלָה זִבְחֵי־צֶדֶק

פָרִים מִזְבַּחֲךָ עַל־ יַעֲלוּ :

References

Psalm 51:0
†2 Sam 12:1

Psalm 51:1
*a*Ps 4:1; 109:26
*b*Ps 69:16; 106:45
*c*Ps 51:9; Is 43:25; 44:22; Acts 3:19; Col 2:14

Psalm 51:2
*a*Ps 51:7; Is 1:16; 4:4; Jer 4:14; Acts 22:16; Rev 1:5
*b*Jer 33:8; Ezek 36:33; Heb 9:14; 1 John 1:7, 9

Psalm 51:3
[1]Or *I myself know*
*a*Is 59:12

Psalm 51:4
[1]Or *may be in the right*
[2]Many mss read *in Your words*
[3]Lit *pure*
*a*Gen 20:6; 39:9; 2 Sam 12:13; Ps 41:4
*b*Luke 15:21
*c*Rom 3:4

Psalm 51:5
*a*Job 14:4; 15:14; Ps 58:3; Eph 2:3

Psalm 51:6
[1]Or *inward parts*
*a*Job 38:36; Ps 15:2
*b*Prov 2:6; Eccl 2:26; James 1:5

Psalm 51:7
[1]Or *May You purify...that I may be clean*
[2]Or *May You wash*
*a*Ex 12:22; Lev 14:4; Num 19:18; Heb 9:19
*b*Is 1:18

Psalm 51:8

[1]Or *May You make*
[a]Is 35:10; Joel 1:16
[b]Ps 35:10

Psalm 51:9
[a]Jer 16:17

Psalm 51:10
[1]Lit *for*
[2]Or *an upright*
[a]Ezek 18:31; Eph 2:10
[b]Ps 24:4; Matt 5:8; Acts 15:9
[c]Ps 78:37

Psalm 51:11
[a]2 Kin 13:23; 24:20; Jer 7:15
[b]Is 63:10, 11

Psalm 51:12
[a]Ps 13:5
[b]Ps 110:3

Psalm 51:13
[1]Or *turn back*
[a]Acts 9:21, 22
[b]Ps 22:27

Psalm 51:14
[a]2 Sam 12:9; Ps 26:9
[b]Ps 25:5
[c]Ps 35:28; 71:15

Psalm 51:15
[1]Or *may You open*
[a]Ex 4:15
[b]Ps 9:14

Psalm 51:16
[a]1 Sam 15:22; Ps 40:6

Psalm 51:17

[a]Ps 34:18

Psalm 51:18
[1]Or *May You build*
[a]Ps 69:35; Is 51:3
[b]Ps 102:16; 147:2

Psalm 51:19
[1]Or *sacrifices of righteousness*
[2]Lit *they will offer young bulls*
[a]Ps 4:5
[b]Ps 66:13, 15

Targum

Psa. 51:1 For praise; a hymn of David.

Psa. 51:2 When Nathan the prophet came to him when he had lain with Bathsheba. [3] Have mercy on me, O LORD, according to your kindness; according to the abundance of your mercies, forgive my rebellion. [4] Cleanse me thoroughly from my iniquity, and make me clean from my sin. [5] For my rebellions are manifest before me, and my sin is in front of me always. [6] Before you, you alone, I have sinned, and that which is evil in your presence I have done; so that you may make me righteous when you speak, you will clear me when you give judgment. [7] Behold, in iniquity was I born, and in sin my mother was pregnant with me. [ANOTHER TARGUM: Behold, in iniquities my father thought to create me; and in the sin of the evil impulse my mother conceived me.] [8] Behold, you desire truth in the inner being ; and in the hidden place of the heart you will make wisdom known. [9] You will sprinkle me like a priest who sprinkles with hyssop waters of purification made from the ashes of the heifer on the unclean, and I will be clean; you will wash me, and I will be whiter than snow. [10] You will proclaim to me joy and jubilation; the limbs that you have purified will rejoice with a hymn. [11] Remove your face from my sins, and blot out all my iniquities. [12] A pure heart create for me, O God; and renew within me a spirit inclined to revere you. [13] Do not cast me from your presence; and do not remove from me your holy spirit of prophecy. [14] Return your Torah to me, to exult in your redemption; and may the spirit of prophecy support me. [15] I will teach the rebellious your ways, and sinners will return to your presence. [16] Deliver me from the sentence of death, O LORD, God of my salvation; my tongue will rejoice in your generosity. [17] O LORD, open my lips with Torah, and my mouth will recount your praise. [18] For you will not desire the holy sacrifice; when I give a burnt offering, you are not pleased. [19] The holy sacrifice of God is a broken spirit; a heart broken and purged, O God, you will not spurn. [20] Show favor in your good will to Zion; you will complete the walls of Jerusalem. [21] Then you will desire the sacrifices of righteousness, burnt offering and holocaust; then the priests will sacrifice bulls on your altar.

Spiritual Awareness

The spiritual rewrite for the verses is in bold.

Introduction

King David had committed adultery and murder because of his lust for Bathsheba. This psalm is his prayer to the LORD for forgiveness. He expresses his repentance for his mistake. Interestingly, in the Prologue of the Sefer Zohar, there is a narrative about David and Bathsheba being soul mates. It says that David had to do what he did to be with his soul mate. The child conceived from the adultress act died just as the prophet Nathan predicted. However, the second child was Solomon. It was Solomon who built the first Temple to the LORD in Jerusalem. That is part of the reasoning behind the Zohar's explanation of the event. It was a sinful event, and David repented. In the Torah, two acts required the death penalty. One was premeditated murder, while the second was adultery. King David committed both. Therefore, it is interesting that the LORD accepted David's repentance.

Superscript

David called upon the Sefirah Netzach for victory over his sins. The prophet Nathan was sent by the LORD to tell David about his sin but, more importantly, to help David repent and return to the LORD's good graces.

To the Sefirah Netzach who grants victory, a psalm of David.

When Nathan the prophet came to him after he had gone to Bathsheba.

Verse one

David turns to the LORD with a plea. He demonstrated his broken spirit and asked for forgiveness. David called upon the Sefirah Chesed for His loving-kindness.

Be gracious to me, O God, from the love of the Sefirah Chesed with full compassion, blot out my transgressions.

Verse two

A transgression is twofold in nature. It is a sin against one's external world and a violation of one's inner purity. David knew well that he sinned when he went to Bathsheba. Then he committed another sin to cover up the first sin. He did not make things better with the coverup. Instead, he made things a lot worse for Bathsheba and himself.

Wash me thoroughly from my sins and cleanse me from my transgression.

Verse three

David admits to his sin. He did not try to deceive himself that what he did was fine. He accepted the responsibility for his transgressions.

For my transgressions are known to me, and my sin is ever before me.

Verse four

The Sages said that David's sin with Bathsheba and his murder of Uriah were violations of the spirit rather than the letter of the legal code of the land (this can be found in the Talmud Shabbos 56b). However, in the sight of the LORD, the crimes were grievous.

Theologians had to determine why David was forgiven for the two capital crimes. Also, the LORD did not remove David from the throne. King Saul consulted with a fortune teller before going into battle against the Philistines, which cost him and his family the throne of Israel. Then David committed two crimes far worse than King Saul's actions, and he was "forgiven." History says that Absolom, David's firstborn son, gathered men together and had an armed revolt. Because of his actions, Absolom wanted to remove his father David from the throne. The revolt did not work.

History says that Solomon took the throne after David. Solomon was the second child of David and Bathsheba. Theologians say that this is additional proof that the LORD forgave him. Was the LORD involved in this part of history, or did He sit back and watch? David was a popular king and built a mighty kingdom. Therefore, the revolt against him did not succeed. So, was it the LORD's intervention, or was the kingdom structure that David built that kept David in power?

Rabbi Steinsaltz said that even though people violate the Torah's different laws, the world continues. In light of that statement projected back to David, the thought is that the LORD did not intervene in the David Bathsheba affair. David broke the law, and life continued. Then a conclusion that follows is the LORD has not been involved with people's daily experiences.

But that goes against what Judaism and Christianity teach. Perhaps it can be said that the LORD influences events through the Sefirot and the Shekinah. Of course, the idea of free choice must be added to the equation. Then Rabbi Steinsaltz's statement about following the Torah works. Each person has the right to choose to follow the Torah. Therefore, David had the free choice to violate the Torah and have an affair with Bathsheba. It would have been up to the kingdom's people to determine if David would have to pay the penalty for his actions. If Abolom's revolt had been successful, then justice for Uriah would have occurred. But the rebellion failed, and Uriah never received justice.

King David was considered the best of the kings. His emblem, the Star of David, symbolizes the Jewish people. So, what the story of David shows is that even the most righteous person is capable of falling into the trap of sin. David saw Bathsheba nude on the top of her home. He liked what he saw and did what he had to do to have her. Even though he knew he was violating the Torah, he did it anyway.

This story is accepted by saying that David was forgiven by the LORD and rewarded. The reward was Solomon and the Temple. Even the Zohar prologue story that David had to marry Bathsheba because they were soulmates is another way to say that the LORD did not intervene. Some theologians would probably say that the death of their firstborn child was a punishment. Losing a child in childbirth is a horrific ordeal. Was that a punishment or a complication of childbirth? Probably today, that child might have been saved.

How much the LORD operates in the world will always be a question. Perhaps one day, an answer will be given to us.

Against You, and against You alone, have I sinned and done that which is evil in Your sight; therefore, You are just in Your speech and pure in Your judgment.

Verses five and six

Augustine could have used verse five to justify his original sin doctrine.

בְּעָווֹן (b'avvon) – means "in inquity." Hirsch says that this word is spelled with two ו; therefore, it means "to commit a sin." Usually, this word has only one ו. The translation of the verse then refers to human nature to commit sin. It is a part of human nature to commit sin. It does not mean that David believed that his conception was sinful. The NASB English translation and other translations have this in their translation.

Behold I was begotten with the capacity to sin, and with a predisposition to iniquity did my mother nurse me.

Behold, however, it is also true that You have directed Your will to that which is hidden by the body and that You teach me wisdom in that which is concealed.

Verse seven

David realized how low he had sunk morally and ethically. He understood the dual nature of humanity. One part is the spark of the LORD, the Neshamah, and the other is the physical body that is a part of the soul. The LORD's purity vs. the flesh's desires is always in conflict. In this situation, David allowed the wishes of his flesh to overwhelm his soul. This problem has plagued humankind from the beginning of the species' existence. The dual nature is introduced in Genesis with Adam and Chava disobeying the LORD and continues throughout history. David prays that the LORD would cleanse him of the sin of his flesh.

Therefore, cleanse me with hyssop so I may be clean; wash me, and I can still become whiter than snow.

Verse eight

David offers his plea to the LORD to regain his physical and spiritual purity. He hoped that he would rise again and have a renewed strength.

Make me hear joy and gladness, let the bones which you have broken rejoice.

Verse nine

David asks the LORD to rebuild their relationship, asking the LORD to forget about his past sins.

Do not view my sins and erase your knowledge of them.

Verse ten

The difference between humans and the rest of the animal kingdom is that humans can make free choices and know what is right or wrong. Humans can use their intellect to control their physical urges and desires. David lost that ability when he took Bathsheba. He asked the LORD to restore him. He used the metaphor of the heart to speak about his spiritual well-being.

Create for me a clean heart, O God, and renew a steadfast spirit within me.

Verse eleven

David was selected by the LORD as a messenger and servant of His work to the Jewish people and the world. David prays that the LORD would not dispose of him like a used tool.

Do not cast me from your presence, and do not take away your Shekinah from me.

Verse twelve

David asked the LORD to help him to rise again to the spiritual purity he had before the incident.

Restore in me the joy of Your salvation, and let the spirit of free devotion uphold me.

Verse thirteen

David said he would teach the people about the LORD's kindness and that sinners can be restored to favor.

Then I will teach sinners Your ways, and men have grown old in sin how they may return to You.

Verse fourteen

The blood guilt is for the two sins David committed that required death. The LORD forgave David. He did not have to die for these sins.

Deliver me from the guilt of blood, O God, God of my victory, so that my tongue may rejoice in the justice of Your loving-kindness.

Verse fifteen

David prayed to reenter the LORD's love.

O LORD, open my lips that my mouth may declare Your praise.

Verse sixteen

Kings did not bring offerings to the LORD.

For You do not demand that I bring sacrifices, and You do not desire burnt offerings.

Verse seventeen

A true offering to the LORD is a spirit broken by the awareness of sin committed.

The sacrifice to God is a broken spirit and a contrite heart, O God, you will not despise.

Verses eighteen and nineteen

There are offerings made to the LORD because of the sins of humans. They serve as a means to help the worshiper in his/her efforts to regain a high moral level and favor with the LORD.

By Your favor, do good to Zion; build the walls of Jerusalem.

Then You will delight in righteous sacrifices, in burnt offerings and whole burnt offerings, then young bulls will be offered on Your altar.

Complete Psalm Rewrite Emphasizing Spiritual Awareness

To the Sefirah Netzach who grants victory, a psalm of David.

When Nathan the prophet came to him after he had gone to Bathsheba.

Be gracious to me, O God, from the love of the Sefirah Chesed with full compassion, blot out my transgressions.

Wash me thoroughly from my sins and cleanse me from my transgression.

For my transgressions are known to me, and my sin is ever before me.

Against You, and against You alone, have I sinned and done that which is evil in Your sight; therefore, You are just in Your speech and pure in Your judgment.

Behold I was begotten with the capacity to sin, and with a predisposition to iniquity did my mother nurse me.

Behold, however, it is also true that You have directed Your will to that which is hidden by the body and that You teach me wisdom in that which is concealed.

Therefore, cleanse me with hyssop so I may be clean; wash me, and I can still become whiter than snow.

Make me hear joy and gladness, let the bones which you have broken rejoice.

Do not view my sins and erase your knowledge of them.

Create for me a clean heart, O God, and renew a steadfast spirit within me.

Do not cast me from your presence, and do not take away your Shekinah from me.

Restore in me the joy of Your salvation, and let the spirit of free devotion uphold me.

Then I will teach sinners Your ways, and men have grown old in sin how they may return to You.

Deliver me from the guilt of blood, O God, God of my victory, so that my tongue may rejoice in the justice of Your loving-kindness.

O LORD, open my lips that my mouth may declare Your praise.

For You do not demand that I bring sacrifices, and You do not desire burnt offerings.

The sacrifice to God is a broken spirit and a contrite heart, O God, you will not despise.

By Your favor, do good to Zion; build the walls of Jerusalem.

Then You will delight in righteous sacrifices, in burnt offerings and whole burnt offerings, then young bulls will be offered on Your altar.

Psalm 52

New American Standard 1995	Hebrew

New American Standard 1995

Psa. 52:0   For the choir director. A †Maskil of David, °when Doeg the Edomite came and told Saul and said to him, "David has come to the house of Ahimelech."

Psa. 52:1   Why do you *a*boast in evil, O mighty man?
  The *b*lovingkindness of God *endures* all day long.
2   Your tongue devises *a*destruction,
  Like a *b*sharp razor, *c*O worker of deceit.
3   You *a*love evil more than good,
  *b*Falsehood more than speaking what is right. [1]Selah.
4   You love all words that devour,
  O *a*deceitful tongue.

Psa. 52:5   [1]But God will break you down forever;
  He will snatch you up and *a*tear you away from *your* tent,
  And *b*uproot you from the [1]land of the living. Selah.
6   The righteous will *a*see and fear,
  And will *b*laugh at him, *saying,*
7   "Behold, the man who would not make God his refuge,
  But *a*trusted in the abundance of his riches
  And *b*was strong in [1]his *evil* desire."

Psa. 52:8   But as for me, I am like a *a*green olive tree in the house of God;

Hebrew

לַמְנַצֵּחַ מַשְׂכִּיל לְדָוִד׃ **Psa. 52:1**

בְּבוֹא ׀ דּוֹאֵג הָאֲדֹמִי **Psa. 52:2**
וַיַּגֵּד לְשָׁאוּל וַיֹּאמֶר לוֹ בָּא דָוִד
אֶל־בֵּית אֲחִימֶלֶךְ׃ 3 מַה־
תִּתְהַלֵּל בְּרָעָה הַגִּבּוֹר חֶסֶד אֵל
כָּל־הַיּוֹם׃ 4 הַוּוֹת תַּחְשֹׁב
לְשׁוֹנֶךָ כְּתַעַר מְלֻטָּשׁ עֹשֵׂה
רְמִיָּה׃ 5 אָהַבְתָּ רָּע מִטּוֹב שֶׁקֶר ׀
מִדַּבֵּר צֶדֶק סֶלָה׃ 6 אָהַבְתָּ
כָל־דִּבְרֵי־בָלַע לָשׁוֹן מִרְמָה׃ 7
גַּם־אֵל יִתָּצְךָ לָנֶצַח יַחְתְּךָ
וְיִסָּחֲךָ מֵאֹהֶל וְשֵׁרֶשְׁךָ מֵאֶרֶץ
חַיִּים סֶלָה׃ 8 וְיִרְאוּ צַדִּיקִים
וְיִירָאוּ וְעָלָיו יִשְׂחָקוּ׃ 9 הִנֵּה
הַגֶּבֶר לֹא יָשִׂים אֱלֹהִים מָעוּזּוֹ
וַיִּבְטַח בְּרֹב עָשְׁרוֹ יָעֹז בְּהַוָּתוֹ׃
10 וַאֲנִי ׀ כְּזַיִת רַעֲנָן בְּבֵית
אֱלֹהִים בָּטַחְתִּי בְחֶסֶד־אֱלֹהִים
עוֹלָם וָעֶד׃ 11 אוֹדְךָ לְעוֹלָם כִּי
עָשִׂיתָ וַאֲקַוֶּה שִׁמְךָ כִי־טוֹב נֶגֶד
חֲסִידֶיךָ׃

I [b]trust in the lovingkindness of God forever and ever. 9 I will [a]give You thanks forever, because You have done *it,* And I will wait on Your name, [b]for *it is* good, in the presence of Your godly ones.	

References

Psalm 52:0
[1]Possibly *Contemplative,* or *Didactic,* or *Skillful Psalm*
[°]1 Sam 22:9

Psalm 52:1
[a]Ps 94:4
[b]Ps 52:8

Psalm 52:2
[a]Ps 5:9
[b]Ps 57:4; 59:7
[c]Ps 101:7

Psalm 52:3
[1]*Selah* may mean: *Pause, Crescendo* or *Musical interlude*
[a]Ps 36:4
[b]Ps 58:3; Jer 9:5

Psalm 52:4
[a]Ps 120:3

Psalm 52:5
[1]Or *Also*
[a]Is 22:18, 19
[b]Prov 2:22
[c]Ps 27:13

Psalm 52:6
[a]Ps 37:34; 40:3
[b]Job 22:19

Psalm 52:7
[1]Or *his destruction*
[a]Ps 49:6
[b]Ps 10:6

Psalm 52:8
[a]Ps 92:12; 128:3; Jer 11:16
[b]Ps 13:5

Targum

Psa. 52:1 For praise; for good teaching; composed by David.

Psa. 52:2 When Doeg the Edomite came and told Saul, and said to him, "David has come to the house of Ahimelech." [3] How the mighty man will praise himself with a wicked tongue, to shed innocent blood; [but] the grace of God is all the day. [4] Your tongue will devise tumult in your heart, forming words of slander like a sharp knife. [5] You love evil more than good, lying more than speaking righteousness always. [6] You love all the words of destruction, the tongue of guile. [7] Also God will demolish you forever; he will shatter you and make you wander so that you cannot dwell in a tent; and he will uproot you from the land of the living forever. [8] And the righteous will see the punishment of the wicked, and they will be afraid in the presence of the LORD, and on his account they will laugh. [9] And they will say, "Behold, the man who did not make the word of the LORD his strength; he trusted in his riches; he was strong in his money." [10] But I, like a luxuriant olive tree in the sanctuary of God, have trusted in the grace of God forever and ever. [11] I will give thanks in your presence forever, for you have accomplished the vindication of my case; and I will await your name, for it is good, before your pious ones.

Spiritual Awareness

The spiritual rewrite for the verses is in bold.

Introduction

This Psalm speaks to the most critical moral problem of David's day. The problem was spreading slander and the fabrication of evil tales to destroy rituals or people. David cites a situation in his life in which this occurred.

David was forced to feel like a beggar because of the jealous wrath of his father-in-law King Saul. During his flight, David was starving and unarmed. He traveled to the city of Nob, where the Tabernacle was located. He spoke with Achimelech, the priest who gave David bread and a sword. Achimelech thought that David was on a conquest for King Saul. Achimelech supplied David with what he needed.

At the same time, Doeg the Edomite, the head of the Sanhedrin, and Saul's closest advisor, went on a spiritual retreat. He went to Nob because the Tabernacle was there. He learned what Achimelech did and reported it to King Saul. He created the rumor that Achimelech was a conspirator against Saul. This incited Saul to condemn the entire city of Nob to death as rebels. Doeg carried out the sentence.

The Edomites and Hebrews were enemies at this time. Therefore, Doeg was a traitor to his people. He believed in the God of Israel and wanted to be a part of the Hebrew nation. Saul elevated him to a position of power that was reserved for men of Israel.

Superscript

David calls to the Sefirah Netzach for victory.

To the Sefirah Netzach and instruction of David, when Doeg the Edomite had come and told Saul, "David has come to the house of Achimelech."

Verse one

How the mighty man will praise himself with a wicked tongue, to shed innocent blood; but the grace of God is all the day.

Verse two

How many times does a person think about the destructive power of speech? Words can hurt like a sharp razor. Doeg created slander that Achimelech assisted David to help David over through Saul. This slander was created by a misunderstanding of circumstances. Doeg wanted Achimelech removed as a priest in Nob, or he did not do his homework to learn why Achimelech assisted David. Today this can be seen when news reports and politicians jump to incorrect conclusions about an event. Facts must be checked and separated from fiction and emotions.

Your tongue devises destruction like a sharp razor, a worker of deceit.

Verse three

David said that Doeg could have discovered the facts when he was in Nob. Doeg could have come before Saul and pleaded David's case. Instead, he created this slander against David and Achimelech. An entire town was destroyed because Doeg was angry with David.

Doeg loved evil more than good, falsehood rather than speaking righteousness. Meditate on this verse.

Verses four & five

David said that Doeg's acts against him and Achimelech showed that Doeg was a dangerous man. Doeg was a person who enjoyed using his words to bring disaster upon innocent people. Doeg represented peril to human happiness. The LORD will send such people away because of their evil influence on others.

But since you are a friend of all devouring words, of the tongue of deceit,

God will also break you forever; He will send you away and remove you far from every tent and uproot you from the land of life. Meditate upon this verse.

Verses six & seven

The Torah could not protect Doeg because he was filled with evil and ungodly arrogance. Evil inclination can build up in a person that even the Torah, positive energy, cannot break through the klippot (the shell that forms around a person filled with evil and is a barrier that prevents goodness from entering the person).

The righteous will see it and be afraid, but they will laugh at him.

Behold the man who did not let God be the source of his strength. He trusted in the abundance of his wealth. Let him be strong, then, by means of what he has devised.

Verse eight

For David, he knew that he had inalienable rights in the House of the LORD. No person can deprive a person of the love of the LORD. Doeg placed his trust in his wealth and position in Saul's court. David put his faith in the mercy of the LORD.

But as for me, I am like the evergreen olive tree in the House of God. I trust in the mercy of God forever.

Verse nine

I will yet give You (God) thanks forever because you have done it, and I will wait upon Your name as it is good unto Your devoted ones.

Complete Psalm Rewrite Emphasizing Spiritual Awareness

To the Sefirah Netzach and instruction of David, when Doeg the Edomite had come and told Saul, "David has come to the house of Achimelech."

How the mighty man will praise himself with a wicked tongue, to shed innocent blood; but the grace of God is all the day.

Your tongue devises destruction like a sharp razor, a worker of deceit.

Doeg loved evil more than good, falsehood rather than speaking righteousness. Meditate on this verse.

But since you are a friend of all devouring words, of the tongue of deceit,

God will also break you forever; He will send you away and remove you far from every tent and uproot you from the land of life. Meditate upon this verse.

The righteous will see it and be afraid, but they will laugh at him.

Behold the man who did not let God be the source of his strength. He trusted in the abundance of his wealth. Let him be strong, then, by means of what he has devised.

But as for me, I am like the evergreen olive tree in the House of God. I trust in the mercy of God forever.

I will yet give You (God) thanks forever because you have done it, and I will wait upon Your name as it is good unto Your devoted ones.

Psalm 53

New American Standard 1995	Hebrew

Psa. 53:1 *a*The fool has said in his heart, "There is no God,"

They are corrupt, and have committed abominable injustice;

*b*There is no one who does good.

2   God has looked down from heaven upon the sons of men

To see if there is *a*anyone who [1]understands,

Who *b*seeks after God.

3   *a*Every one of them has turned aside; together they have become corrupt;

There is no one who does good, not even one.

Psa. 53:4 Have the workers of wickedness *a*no knowledge,

Who eat up My people *as though* they ate bread

And have not called upon God?

5   There they were in great [1]fear *a*where no [1]fear had been;

For God *b*scattered the bones of [2]him who encamped against you;

You *c*put *them* to shame, because *d*God had rejected them.

6   Oh, that *a*the salvation of Israel [1]would come out of Zion!

When God [2]restores His captive people,

[3]Let Jacob rejoice, let Israel be glad.

הַשְׁכֵּיל עַל־מָחֲלַת לַמְנַצֵּחַ **Psa. 53:1**

אֵין בְּלִבּוֹ נָבָל אָמַר 2 :לְדָוִד

אֵין עָוֶל וְהִתְעִיבוּ הִשְׁחִיתוּ אֱלֹהִים

מִשָּׁמַיִם אֱלֹהִים 3 :טוֹב־עֹשֵׂה

הֲיֵשׁ לִרְאוֹת אָדָם עַל־בְּנֵי הִשְׁקִיף

כֻּלּוֹ 4 :אֱלֹהִים אֶת־דֹּרֵשׁ מַשְׂכִּיל

אֵין טוֹב־עֹשֵׂה אֵין נֶאֱלָחוּ יַחְדָּו סָג

אָוֶן פֹּעֲלֵי יָדְעוּ הֲלֹא 5 :אֶחָד גַּם־

לֹא אֱלֹהִים לֶחֶם אָכְלוּ עַמִּי אֹכְלֵי

לֹא־פַחַד פָּחֲדוּ שָׁם 6 :קָרָאוּ

עַצְמוֹת פִּזַּר כִּי־אֱלֹהִים פַחַד הָיָה

7 :מְאָסָם כִּי־אֱלֹהִים הֱבִשֹׁתָה חֹנָךְ

בְּשׁוּב יִשְׂרָאֵל יְשׁוּעוֹת מִצִּיּוֹן יִתֵּן מִי

יַעֲקֹב יָגֵל עַמּוֹ שְׁבוּת אֱלֹהִים

:יִשְׂרָאֵל יִשְׂמַח

References

Psalm 53:0
I.e. sickness, a sad tone
°Possibly *Contemplative,* or *Didactic,* or *Skillful Psalm*

Psalm 53:1
[a]Ps 10:4; 14:1-7; 53:1-6
[b]Rom 3:10

Psalm 53:2
[1]Or *acts wisely*
[a]Rom 3:11
[b]2 Chr 15:2

Psalm 53:3
[a]Rom 3:12

Psalm 53:4
[a]Jer 4:22

Psalm 53:5
[1]Or *dread*
[2]Or possibly *those*
[a]Lev 26:17, 36; Prov 28:1
[b]Ps 141:7; Jer 8:1, 2; Ezek 6:5
[c]Ps 44:7
[d]2 Kin 17:20; Jer 6:30; Lam 5:22

Psalm 53:6
[1]Lit *would be*
[2]Or *restores the fortunes of His people*
[3]Or *Jacob will rejoice, Israel will be glad*
[a]Ps 14:7**Targum**

Spiritual Awareness

The spiritual rewrite for the verses are in bold.

Introduction

Psalm 53 is an almost exact replica of Psalm 14. Psalm 14 is believed to be about the destruction of the first Temple, while Psalm 53 is about the destruction of the second Temple. Since David wrote this Psalm, it was a prediction that David made. Since it came to pass, this proves that David had prophetic gifts from the LORD.

The establishment of the House of David was not an easy task. Besides Saul and his family trying to stop David, several nations surrounding Israel did not want it to happen. Saul was weak in foreign policy, and David was viewed as being strong. The LORD established David on the throne of Israel, and his descendants were to be on the throne until the day of the Messiah. On that day, any exile of the Jewish people would terminate. However, the Psalm says that the Messiah will suffer persecution at the hands of skeptics and scoffers.

This is a problem for Jews to accept Jesus of Nazareth as more than a prophet. The traditions outlined in this Psalm and in other writings indicate the vindication of Israel with an end to foreign rule, just to mention one item. This did not happen when Jesus of Nazareth was born. Jesus was born in Galilee. That places doubts on his being a part of the line of David. Jews in Judea at that time did not view Galileans nor Samaritans as Jews.

Superscript

מָחֲלַת (Mahalat*)* - "This technical musical term of uncertain meaning is found in the headings of Ps 53 and 88 [H 53:1 and 88:1]. Most [Vol. 1, p. 288] versions transliterate the term. The NASB suggests a connection with חָלָה "to be weak, sick," hence a sad tune. Others relate it to מְחֹלָה, a round dance. In Ps 88, where it is joined with "Leannoth," the NIV says it may possibly be a tune, "The Suffering of Affliction." For other such terms see סֶלָה."[1]

נַצֵּחַ (Natacha) – this word is the name of the Sefirah Netzach. This Sefirah offers victory to the people who call upon its name.

To Netzach who grants victory over widespread infirmity, an instruction by David.

Verse 1

Psalm 14 voiced a faith that has sustained Israel since its inception. This faith has kept the Hebrew people together throughout its long period of destitution.

נָבָל (naval) verb, be senseless, foolish. It can also be translated as "withered." History has shown that humans enter a time of mental and moral degradation whenever they become foolish.

Israel's enemies called them foolish for their faith and hope in the LORD. As long as Israel kept their covenant with the LORD, they were always protected. נָבָל denotes

---

[1] R. Laird Harris, Gleason L. Archer, and Bruce K. Waltke, "Theological Wordbook of The Old Testament (1980 Edition)," Open Library (Moody Press, January 1, 1980), https://openlibrary.org/books/OL4112955M/Theological_wordbook_of_the_Old_Testament.

the disappearance of unfettered moral strength. The nation was "going down the tubes," and it appeared that no one could stop it.

In his heart, the foolish man has said, "There is no God"; they are corrupt and an abomination because their activities are not those of a person who wants to do good.

Verse 2

Humans who deny the existence of the LORD do so because the LORD cannot be detected by reason.

The LORD observes from Heaven to find humans who are searching for Him by using their reason.

Verse 3

The author believed that every person was corrupt and had turned away from the LORD. Therefore, the LORD does not need to intervene and bring punishment to the people because every member of society serves as a punishment for his/her fellow citizens. In other words, the people punish each other by their violence toward each other.

There have often been periods when all humanity seemed to be corrupted, and no one did anything good.

All humanity is depraved. No one is doing anything good, not a single person.

Verse 4

Even when it appears that all humanity is corrupt and perverted, there has always been a nation that respected the LORD and obeyed His divine law. That nation is Israel. Without Israel, the world would have become completely lost.

The doers of violence do not know who devours Israel like a person eating bread and has not invited the LORD?

Verse 5

The people who transgressed against the people of Israel learned about divine justice.

There they were in great fear where no fear had been; For God scattered the bones of him who encamped against you; You put them to shame, because God had rejected them.

Verse 6

Salvation is a gift given to Israel by the LORD.

Oh, that the salvation of Israel would come out of Zion! When God restores His captive people, Let Jacob rejoice, let Israel be glad.

Complete Psalm Rewrite Emphasizing Spiritual Awareness

To Netzach who grants victory over widespread infirmity, an instruction by David.

In his heart, the foolish man has said, "There is no God"; they are corrupt and an abomination because their activities are not those of a person who wants to do good.

The LORD observes from Heaven to find humans who are searching for Him by using their reason.

All humanity is depraved. No one is doing anything good, not a single person. The doers of violence do not know who devours Israel like a person eating bread and has not invited the LORD?

There they were in great fear where no fear had been; For God scattered the bones of him who encamped against you; You put them to shame, because God had rejected them.
Oh, that the salvation of Israel would come out of Zion! When God restores His captive people, Let Jacob rejoice, let Israel be glad.

Psalm 54

New American Standard 1995	Hebrew

New American Standard 1995

Psa. 54:0 For the choir director; on stringed instruments. A †Maskil of David, °when the Ziphites came and said to Saul, "Is not David hiding himself among us?"

Psa. 54:1   Save me, O God, by *a*Your name,
And ¹vindicate me by *b*Your power.
2   *a*Hear my prayer, O God;
*b*Give ear to the words of my mouth.
3   For strangers have *a*risen against me
And *b*violent men have *c*sought my ¹life;
They have *d*not set God before them.
²Selah.

Psa. 54:4   Behold, *a*God is my helper;
The Lord is ¹the *b*sustainer of my soul.
5   ¹He will *a*recompense the evil to ²my foes;
³*b*Destroy them *c*in Your ⁴faithfulness.

Psa. 54:6   ¹*a*Willingly I will sacrifice to You;
I will give *b*thanks to Your name, O LORD, for it is good.
7   For ¹He has *a*delivered me from all ²trouble,
And my eye has *b*looked *with satisfaction* upon my enemies.

Hebrew

Psa. 54:1 לַמְנַצֵּחַ בִּנְגִינֹת מַשְׂכִּיל
לְדָוִד׃

Psa. 54:2 בְּבוֹא הַזִּיפִים וַיֹּאמְרוּ
לְשָׁאוּל הֲלֹא דָוִד מִסְתַּתֵּר עִמָּנוּ׃ 3
אֱלֹהִים בְּשִׁמְךָ הוֹשִׁיעֵנִי וּבִגְבוּרָתְךָ
תְדִינֵנִי׃ 4 אֱלֹהִים שְׁמַע תְּפִלָּתִי
הַאֲזִינָה לְאִמְרֵי־פִי׃ 5 כִּי זָרִים ׀
קָמוּ עָלַי וְעָרִיצִים בִּקְשׁוּ נַפְשִׁי לֹא
שָׂמוּ אֱלֹהִים לְנֶגְדָּם סֶלָה׃ 6 הִנֵּה
אֱלֹהִים עֹזֵר לִי אֲדֹנָי בְּסֹמְכֵי
נַפְשִׁי׃ 7 יָשׁוֹב [יָשִׁיב] הָרַע לְשֹׁרְרָי
בַּאֲמִתְּךָ הַצְמִיתֵם׃ 8 בִּנְדָבָה
אֶזְבְּחָה־לָּךְ אוֹדֶה שִּׁמְךָ יְהוָה כִּי־
טוֹב׃ 9 כִּי מִכָּל־צָרָה הִצִּילָנִי
וּבְאֹיְבַי רָאֲתָה עֵינִי׃

References

Psalm 54:0
†Possibly *Contemplative,* or *Didactic,* or *Skillful Psalm*
°1 Sam 23:19; 26:1

Psalm 54:1
1Lit *judge*
aPs 20:1
b2 Chr 20:6

Psalm 54:2
aPs 17:6; 55:1
bPs 5:1

Psalm 54:3
1Or *soul*
2*Selah* may mean: *Pause, Crescendo* or *Musical interlude*
aPs 86:14
bPs 18:48; 86:14; 140:1, 4, 11
c1 Sam 20:1; 25:29; Ps 40:14; 63:9; 70:2
dPs 36:1

Psalm 54:4
1Lit *as those who sustain*
aPs 30:10; 37:40; 118:7
bPs 37:17, 24; 41:12; 51:12; 145:14; Is 41:10

Psalm 54:5
1Lit *The evil will return*
2Or *those who lie in wait for me*
3Or *Put to silence*
4Or *truth*
aPs 94:23
bPs 143:12
cPs 89:49; 96:13; Is 42:3

Psalm 54:6
1Or *With a freewill offering*
aNum 15:3; Ps 116:17
bPs 50:14

Psalm 54:7
1Or *it;* i.e. His name
2Or *distress*
aPs 34:6
bPs 59:10; 92:11; 112:8; 118:7

Targum

Psa. 54:1 For praise, with a hymn. Good teaching composed by David.

Psa. 54:2 When the men of Ziph came and said to Saul, "Is not David hiding with us?" [3] O God, by your name redeem me, and by the strength of your might judge me. [4] O LORD, accept my prayer; listen to the utterance of my mouth. [5] For arrogant men have risen against me, and powerful men have sought my life; they have not put God before them forever. [6] Behold, the LORD is my helper, the LORD is among the supports of my soul. [7] May evil return to those who oppress me; in your faithfulness bring them low. [8] With an offering I will sacrifice in your presence; I will give thanks to your name, O LORD, for it is good. [9] For he has delivered me from every trouble; and my eye has seen vengeance against my enemies.

Spiritual Awareness

The spiritual rewrite for the verses is in bold.

Introduction

An entire community is ruined by gossip, according to this Psalm. The treachery of the Ziphites surpassed Doeg from Psalm 53. These people were from the tribe of Judah. Therefore, they were relatives of David. They betrayed David to King Saul. Saul was surprised that any Judeans would betray David, who was from the tribe of Judah.

Superscript

This Psalm was written to the Sefirah Netzah, who gives victory through the power of music.

To the Sefirah Netzach, who grants victory through the power of music, an instrument of David, when the Ziphites came and said to Saul, "Is not David hiding among us?"

Verse one

David was fleeing from his father-in-law King Saul. He was forced to live in the woods because he was betrayed by his fellow tribesmen. David appealed to the LORD for the qualities of Divine sovereignty and hope for salvation.

O God, grant me salvation by Your Name, and champion my right by Your might.

Verse two

David calls upon the LORD's justice.

Hear my prayer; incline Your ear to the words of my mouth.

Verse three

כִּי זָרִים | קָמוּ עָלַי (key zarim kamu ala) – means "for strangers have risen against me." These men with whom David never had any dealings before and therefore have no reason to be his enemies, yet they are after him. David wondered why his own brothers of Judah were trying to kill him.

For strangers have risen against me, and bold men have sought my soul; they have not set God before themselves.

Verse Four

David believed that the justice of the LORD's sovereignty stood by his side. This reassured David that he would survive because the LORD appointed him to lead Israel.

Behold, God is at my side, my Master, through those who uphold my soul.

Verse five

David believed that the people helping Saul to kill him had to create false faults in him. They were being controlled by Evil Inclination.

He will repay the evil to those that lie in wait for me; make them numb by Your truth.

Verses six and seven

David envisions himself before the LORD. He pledges himself to the LORD, who he knew would save him.

I shall bring sacrifices unto You with devotion; I shall acknowledge You, God, that He is the Good one.

How He has delivered me out of all trouble and how my eye has seen this in the case of my enemies.

Complete Psalm Rewrite Emphasizing Spiritual Awareness

O God, grant me salvation by Your Name, and champion my right by Your might.

Hear my prayer; incline Your ear to the words of my mouth.

For strangers have risen against me, and bold men have sought my soul; they have not set God before themselves.

Behold, God is at my side, my Master, through those who uphold my soul.

He will repay the evil to those that lie in wait for me; make them numb by Your truth.

I shall bring sacrifices unto You with devotion; I shall acknowledge You, God, that He is the Good one.

How He has delivered me out of all trouble and how my eye has seen this in the case of my enemies.

Psalm 55

New American Standard 1995	Hebrew
Psa. 55:1 [a]Give ear to my prayer, O God; And [b]do not hide Yourself from my supplication. 2 Give [a]heed to me and answer me; I am restless in my [b]complaint and [1c]am surely distracted, 3 Because of the voice of the enemy, Because of the [a]pressure of the wicked; For they [b]bring down [1]trouble upon me And in anger they [c]bear a grudge against me. **Psa. 55:4** My [a]heart is in anguish within me, And the terrors of [b]death have fallen upon me. 5 Fear and [a]trembling come upon me, And [1b]horror has overwhelmed me. 6 I said, "Oh, that I had wings like a dove! I would fly away and [1a]be at rest. 7 "Behold, I would wander far away, I would [a]lodge in the wilderness. [1]Selah. 8 "I would hasten to my place of refuge From the [a]stormy wind *and* tempest." **Psa. 55:9** [1]Confuse, O Lord, [a]divide their tongues,	**Psa. 55:1** לַמְנַצֵּחַ בִּנְגִינֹת מַשְׂכִּיל לְדָוִד ׃ 2 הַאֲזִינָה אֱלֹהִים תְּפִלָּתִי וְאַל־ תִּתְעַלַּם מִתְּחִנָּתִי ׃ 3 הַקְשִׁיבָה לִּי וַעֲנֵנִי אָרִיד בְּשִׂיחִי וְאָהִימָה ׃ 4 מִקּוֹל אוֹיֵב מִפְּנֵי עָקַת רָשָׁע כִּי־ יָמִיטוּ עָלַי אָוֶן וּבְאַף יִשְׂטְמוּנִי ׃ 5 לִבִּי יָחִיל בְּקִרְבִּי וְאֵימוֹת מָוֶת נָפְלוּ עָלָי ׃ 6 יִרְאָה וָרַעַד יָבֹא בִי וַתְּכַסֵּנִי פַּלָּצוּת ׃ 7 וָאֹמַר מִי־יִתֶּן־לִי אֵבֶר כַּיּוֹנָה אָעוּפָה וְאֶשְׁכֹּנָה ׃ 8 הִנֵּה אַרְחִיק נְדֹד אָלִין בַּמִּדְבָּר סֶלָה ׃ 9 אָחִישָׁה מִפְלָט לִי מֵרוּחַ סֹעָה מִסָּעַר ׃ 10 בַּלַּע אֲדֹנָי פַּלַּג לְשׁוֹנָם כִּי־רָאִיתִי חָמָס וְרִיב בָּעִיר ׃ 11 יוֹמָם וָלַיְלָה יְסוֹבְבֻהָ עַל־חוֹמֹתֶיהָ

For I have seen [b]violence and strife in the city.

10 Day and night they go around her upon her walls,

And iniquity and mischief are in her midst.

11 [a]Destruction is in her midst;

[b]Oppression and deceit do not depart from her [1]streets.

Psa. 55:12 For it is [a]not an enemy who reproaches me,

Then I could bear *it*;

Nor is it one who hates me who [b]has exalted himself against me,

Then I could hide myself from him.

13 But it is you, a man [1]my equal,

My [a]companion and my [2b]familiar friend;

14 We who had sweet [1]fellowship together

[a]Walked in the house of God in the throng.

15 Let [1]death come [a]deceitfully upon them;

Let them [b]go down alive to [2]Sheol,

For evil is in their dwelling, in their midst.

Psa. 55:16 As for me, I shall [a]call upon God,

And the LORD will save me.

17 [a]Evening and [b]morning and at [c]noon, I will complain and murmur,

And He will hear my voice.

18 He will [a]redeem my soul in peace [1]from the battle *which is* against me,

For they are [b]many *who strive* with me.

וְאָ֥וֶן וְעָמָ֗ל בְּקִרְבָּֽהּ׃ 12 הַוֺּ֥ות בְּקִרְבָּ֑הּ וְֽלֹא־יָמִ֥ישׁ מֵ֝רְחֹבָ֗הּ תֹּ֥ךְ וּמִרְמָֽה׃ 13 כִּ֤י לֹֽא־אֹויֵ֡ב יְחָרְפֵ֗נִי וְאֶשָּׂ֫א לֹא־מְשַׂנְאִ֥י עָלַ֥י הִגְדִּ֑יל וְאֶסָּתֵ֥ר מִמֶּֽנּוּ׃ 14 וְאַתָּ֣ה אֱנֹ֣ושׁ כְּעֶרְכִּ֑י אַ֝לּוּפִ֗י וּמְיֻדָּעִֽי׃ 15 אֲשֶׁ֣ר יַ֭חְדָּו נַמְתִּ֣יק סֹ֑וד בְּבֵ֥ית אֱ֝לֹהִ֗ים נְהַלֵּ֥ךְ בְּרָֽגֶשׁ׃ 16 יַשִּׁ֤ימָ֘וֶת [יַשִּׁ֪י] [מָ֪וֶת] עָלֵ֗ימֹו יֵרְד֣וּ שְׁאֹ֣ול חַיִּ֑ים כִּֽי־רָעֹ֖ות בִּמְגוּרָ֣ם בְּקִרְבָּֽם׃ 17 אֲנִ֗י אֶל־אֱלֹהִ֥ים אֶקְרָ֑א וַֽ֝יהוָ֗ה יֹושִׁיעֵֽנִי׃ 18 עֶ֤רֶב וָבֹ֣קֶר וְ֭צָהֳרַיִם אָשִׂ֣יחָה וְאֶהֱמֶ֑ה וַיִּשְׁמַ֥ע קֹולִֽי׃ 19 פָּ֘דָ֤ה בְשָׁלֹ֣ום נַ֭פְשִׁי מִקֲּרָב־לִ֑י כִּֽי־בְ֝רַבִּ֗ים הָי֥וּ עִמָּדִֽי׃ 20 יִשְׁמַ֤ע ׀ אֵ֨ל ׀ וְֽיַעֲנֵם֮ וְיֹ֤שֵׁ֫ב קֶ֥דֶם סֶ֑לָה אֲשֶׁ֤ר אֵ֣ין חֲלִיפֹ֣ות לָ֑מֹו וְלֹ֖א יָרְא֣וּ אֱלֹהִֽים׃ 21 שָׁלַ֣ח יָ֭דָיו בִּשְׁלֹמָ֗יו חִלֵּ֥ל בְּרִיתֹֽו׃ 22 חָלְק֤וּ ׀ מַחְמָאֹ֬ת

19 God will *hear and ¹answer them —

Even the one *who ²sits enthroned from of old — Selah.
With whom there ³is no change,
And who *do not fear God.

20 He has put forth his hands against *those who were at peace with him;
He has ¹*violated his covenant.

21 His ¹speech was *smoother than butter,
But his heart was war;
His words were *softer than oil,
Yet they were drawn *swords.

Psa. 55:22 *Cast ¹your burden upon the LORD and He will sustain you;
*He will never allow the righteous to ²*be shaken.

23 But You, O God, will bring them down to the ¹*pit of destruction;
*Men of bloodshed and deceit will *not live out half their days.
But I will *trust in You.

פִּיו וְקְרָב־לִבּוֹ רַכּוּ דְבָרָיו
מִשֶּׁמֶן וְהֵמָּה פְתִחֹות ׃ 23
הַשְׁלֵךְ עַל־יְהוָה וִיהָבְךָ
וְהוּא יְכַלְכְּלֶךָ לֹא־יִתֵּן
לְעוֹלָם מוֹט לַצַּדִּיק ׃ 24
וְאַתָּה אֱלֹהִים תּוֹרִדֵם
לִבְאֵר שַׁחַת אַנְשֵׁי דָמִים
וּמִרְמָה לֹא־יֶחֱצוּ יְמֵיהֶם
וַאֲנִי אֶבְטַח־בָּךְ ׃

References

Psalm 55:0
[1]Possibly *Contemplative,* or *Didactic,* or *Skillful Psalm*

Psalm 55:1
[a]Ps 54:2; 61:1; 86:6
[b]Ps 27:9

Psalm 55:2
[1]Or *I must moan*
[a]Ps 66:19; 86:6, 7
[b]1 Sam 1:16; Job 9:27; Ps 64:1; 77:3; 142:2
[c]Is 38:14; 59:11; Ezek 7:16

Psalm 55:3
[1]Or *wickedness*
[a]Ps 17:9
[b]2 Sam 16:7, 8
[c]Ps 71:11; 143:3

Psalm 55:4
[a]Ps 38:8
[b]Ps 18:4, 5; 116:3

Psalm 55:5
[1]Lit *shuddering*
[a]Ps 119:120
[b]Job 21:6; Is 21:4; Ezek 7:18

Psalm 55:6
[1]Lit *settle down*
[a]Job 3:13

Psalm 55:7
[1]*Selah* may mean: *Pause, Crescendo* or *Musical interlude*
[a]1 Sam 23:14

Psalm 55:8
[a]Is 4:6; 25:4; 29:6

Psalm 55:9

[1]Lit *Swallow up*
[a]Gen 11:9
[b]Ps 11:5; Jer 6:7

Psalm 55:11
[1]Or *plaza*
[a]Ps 5:9
[b]Ps 10:7; 17:9

Psalm 55:12
[a]Ps 41:9
[b]Ps 35:26

Psalm 55:13
[1]Lit *according to my valuation*
[2]Or *acquaintance*
[a]2 Sam 15:12
[b]Job 19:14; Ps 41:9

Psalm 55:14
[1]Lit *counsel;* or *intimacy*
[a]Ps 42:4

Psalm 55:15
[1]Another reading is *desolations be upon them*
[2]I.e. the nether world
[a]Ps 64:7; Prov 6:15; Is 47:11; 1 Thess 5:3
[b]Num 16:30, 33

Psalm 55:16
[a]Ps 57:2, 3

Psalm 55:17
[a]Ps 141:2; Dan 6:10; Acts 3:1; 10:3, 30
[b]Ps 5:3; 88:13; 92:2
[c]Acts 10:9

Psalm 55:18
[1]Or *so that none may approach me*
[a]Ps 103:4
[b]Ps 56:2

Psalm 55:19

[1]Or *afflict*
[2]Or *abides from*
[3]Lit *are no changes*
[a]Ps 78:59
[b]Deut 33:27; Ps 90:2; 93:2
[c]Ps 36:1

Psalm 55:20

[1]Lit *profaned*
[a]Ps 7:4; 120:7
[b]Num 30:2; Ps 89:34

Psalm 55:21

[1]Lit *mouth*
[a]Ps 12:2; 28:3; Prov 5:3, 4
[b]Ps 57:4; 59:7

Psalm 55:22

[1]Or *what He has given you*
[2]Or *totter*
[a]Ps 37:5; 1 Pet 5:7
[b]Ps 37:24
[c]Ps 15:5; 112:6

Psalm 55:23

[1]Or *lowest pit*
[a]Ps 73:18; Is 38:17; Ezek 28:8
[b]Ps 5:6
[c]Job 15:32; Prov 10:27
[d]Ps 25:2; 56:3

Targum

Psa. 55:1 For praise, with the words of a hymn; good teaching composed by David. [2] Hear, O God, my prayer, and do not hide yourself from my prayer. [3] Hear my utterance, and accept it from me; I will roar out in my words and be agitated. [4] From the voice of the enemy, from the trouble of the wicked, for they extend lies against me, and in anger they will hold a grudge towards me. [5] My heart will tremble within me, and the terrors of death have fallen upon me. [6] Fear and trembling come to me, and disaster has covered me. [7] And I said, "Who will give to me wings like a dove, [that] I may fly and come to rest?" [8] Behold, I would go to a far place to wander, I would lodge in the wilderness forever. [9] I would make hasten to me rescue from the tempest, shelter from the storm. [10] Destroy, O LORD, their counsel, divide their tongue, for I have seen violence and strife in the city. [11] Day and night they encircle it, around her walls, and misery and lies are in her midst. [12] Tumult is in her midst, and lies and deceit do not depart from her squares. [13] For an enemy will not belittle me, else I would bear it; my foe has not vaunted himself against me, else I would hide from his presence. [14] But you, O Achitophel, a man who is like me; a leader who taught me, and who tells me wisdom. [15] For together we will explain mysteries in the sanctuary of God, we will walk in haste. [16] He will condemn them to the judgement of death, and he will decree for them evil things, for Doeg and Achitophel; they will descend to Sheol while alive, for evil things are in their dwellings, in their bodies. [17] I will pray in the presence of God, and the word of the LORD will redeem me. [18] In the evening, and in the morning, and at noon I will pray, and I will tremble; and he heard my voice. [19] He redeemed my soul in peace, so that no evil came near to me, for his word was my help in many troubles. [20] God will hear and receive from them [their prayer], and the one who dwells in heaven from of old forever; but the wicked who are not from of old, who do not change their ways, are evil, and are not afraid in the presence of God. [21] He stretched out his hands against the men of his peace; he desecrated his covenant. [22] Smoother than oil of curds are the words of his mouth; and like weapons of war his heart. Softer are his words than tallow, but they are deadly lances. [23] Cast your confidence on the LORD, and he will feed you; he will never allow privation to the righteous. [24] But you, O God, by your word will bring them down to deep Gehenna; murderous and deceitful men will not see half of their days; but I will trust in your word.

Spiritual Awareness

The spiritual rewrite for the verses is in bold.

Introduction

The setting for this Psalm is Absalom's rebellion against his father, King David. David was puzzled that Achotifel became Absalom's primary supporter. Achotifel was a friend and advisor of David. David's most intimate companion, whom he revered as a teacher, had turned against him.

Superscript

To the Sefirah Netzach who grants victory through the power of music, an instruction by David.

Verse one

David turned to the LORD as he strived for clarity of thought. He was trying to understand why Achotifel turned against him.

Hear, O God, my prayer, and please do not leave me.

Verse two

David said that he was agitated about the circumstances he found himself in.

Attend me and answer me, for I am sad in my meditation, and my anger grows.

Verses three, four, five

מִקָּוֹל (meekol) – literally means "to waver." Since it is in its noun form, it denotes "a suspended device for carrying." A stretcher would be such a device.

Because of the raging of the foe, because of the oppression of the lawless; for they charge me with the misuse of my power, and with outward show anger they hate me bitterly in their innards.

Therefore my heart writhes within me, and the terrors of death have fallen upon me.

Fear and trembling overpower me as horror overcomes me.

Verses six, seven, eight

In these verses, David exclaims that he wished he could have fled from Absalom.

And I said, I that I had wings like the dove! Then I would fly away and find a place of rest.

Behold then, I would wander far off and dwell in the wilderness. Meditate on this verse.

I would quickly devise deliverance for myself from the stormy wind that draws nigh and from the tempest.

Verses nine, ten, eleven

These verses explain why David had to endure so many troubles in his life. The verses develop an indictment against a specific enemy.

Subdue, O God, and divide their tongue, for I have seen only violence and strife in the city.

Day and night, they go about it upon its walls, and iniquity and disaster are in the midst of it.

Plots are hatched within it, and malice and deceit depart not from its open spaces.

Verse twelve

David's despair is shown in this verse. The widespread corruption in his administration was unbearable. His main despair was how Achitofel, a man of high esteem, could turn on David and spread lies. Achitofel became disloyal to David. He agonized over this for the rest of his life.

For it is not an enemy that reviles me, else I could have borne it; neither was it, the usual adversary that magnified himself against me, else I would have hidden from him.

Verse thirteen

David entrusted Achitofel with his inner secrets and feelings. Achitofel was never guilty of arrogance. However, he had turned on David.

But it was you, a mortal, my equal, my guide, and my familiar friend.

Verse fourteen

David describes the relationship between Achitofel and himself.

Together we kept the sweet secret; we walk into the House of God when there is turmoil outside.

Verse fifteen

God appoints death to collect the debt from the rebels. It was pretty sudden.

He appoints death to collect the debt they owe; they go down alive to the grave, for they bear the evil within themselves in their temporal dwelling place.

Verse sixteen

Achitofel taught David to always trust the LORD.

As for me, I will call upon God, and because He is the LORD, he will save me.

Verse seventeen

Despite the inner turmoil that David was feeling, he needed to muster the strength for prayer.

When I pray in the evening and morning and noonday, and I am restless, He has already heard my voice.

Verse eighteen

David acknowledged that every peaceful and happy day he ever felt was a gift from the LORD.

Even in times of peace, it was He alone Who redeemed my soul from impending struggle, even when there were many that stood at my side.

Verse nineteen

David believed that the LORD intervened in human events against the godless and those who refuted their exaggerated claims. Since the LORD does not seem to reveal His might by direct intervention in the course of human destinies, they believe there can be no change in their fortunes. These persons forget to revere the LORD. If the LORD intervened, then David must have wondered why the struggle against the rebellion was not halted by the LORD.

God will hear them and will give them their answer, though, as in days long past, He may sit upon His throne so that they neither believe in change nor fear God.

Verse twenty

The words and utterances by Achitofel are being used by him. He did a violence that he protested against.

And how he has put forth his hands against his own protestations of peace; he has profaned his own covenant.

Verse Twenty-one

מַחְמָאֹת (mach'maot) – means "butter." The phrase smooth as butter refers to anything that is smooth and soft.

Smooth as butter were the words of his mouth, but he bore war within his heart. Softer than oil were his words, and yet they were drawn swords.

Verse Twenty-two, twenty-three

David knew that the followers of Achitofel would bring their own destruction.

Cast upon God what has been placed upon you; He will provide for you. He will never allow the righteous to waver.

But you, O God, will throw them into the well of destruction; men of bloodguilt and deceit shall not live out half their days; but as for me, I shall trust in You.

Complete Psalm Rewrite Emphasizing Spiritual Awareness

To the Sefirah Netzach who grants victory through the power of music, an instruction by David.

Hear, O God, my prayer, and please do not leave me.

Attend me and answer me, for I am sad in my meditation, and my anger grows.

Because of the raging of the foe, because of the oppression of the lawless; for they charge me with the misuse of my power, and with outward show anger they hate me bitterly in their innards.

Therefore my heart writhes within me, and the terrors of death have fallen upon me.

Fear and trembling overpower me as horror overcomes me.

And I said, I that I had wings like the dove! Then I would fly away and find a place of rest.

Behold then, I would wander far off and dwell in the wilderness. Meditate on this verse.

I would quickly devise deliverance for myself from the stormy wind that draws nigh and from the tempest.

Subdue, O God, and divide their tongue, for I have seen only violence and strife in the city.

Day and night, they go about it upon its walls, and iniquity and disaster are in the midst of it.

Plots are hatched within it, and malice and deceit depart not from its open spaces.

For it is not an enemy that reviles me, else I could have borne it; neither was it, the usual adversary that magnified himself against me, else I would have hidden from him.

But it was you, a mortal, my equal, my guide, and my familiar friend.

Together we kept the sweet secret; we walk into the House of God when there is turmoil outside.

He appoints death to collect the debt they owe; they go down alive to the grave, for they bear the evil within themselves in their temporal dwelling place.

As for me, I will call upon God, and because He is the LORD, he will save me.

When I pray in the evening and morning and noonday, and I am restless, He has already heard my voice.

Even in times of peace, it was He alone Who redeemed my soul from impending struggle, even when there were many that stood at my side.

God will hear them and will give them their answer, though, as in days long past, He may sit upon His throne so that they neither believe in change nor fear God.

And how he has put forth his hands against his own protestations of peace; he has profaned his own covenant.

Smooth as butter were the words of his mouth, but he bore war within his heart. Softer than oil were his words, and yet they were drawn swords.

Cast upon God what has been placed upon you; He will provide for you. He will never allow the righteous to waver.

But you, O God, will throw them into the well of destruction; men of bloodguilt and deceit shall not live out half their days; but as for me, I shall trust in You.

Psalm 56

New American Standard 1995	Hebrew

Psa. 56:0   For the choir director; according to †Jonath elem rehokim. A °Mikhtam of David, ^when the Philistines seized him in Gath.

Psa. 56:1   Be gracious to me, O God, for man has [1a]trampled upon me;

[2]Fighting all day long he [b]oppresses me.

2   My foes have [1a]trampled upon me all day long,

For [2]they are many who [b]fight proudly against me.

3   [1]When I am [a]afraid,

[2]I will [b]put my trust in You.

4   [a]In God, whose word I praise,

In God I have put my trust;

I shall not be afraid.

[b]What can *mere* [1]man do to me?

5   All day long they [1a]distort my words;

All their [2b]thoughts are against me for evil.

6   They [1a]attack, they lurk,

They [b]watch my [2]steps,

As they have [c]waited *to take* my [3]life.

7   Because of wickedness, [1a]cast them forth,

In anger [b]put down the peoples, O God!

Psa. 56:8   You [a]have taken account of my wanderings;

Put my [b]tears in Your bottle.

לַמְנַצֵּחַ ׀ עַל־יוֹנַת אֵלֶם **Psa. 56:1**
רְחֹקִים לְדָוִד מִכְתָּם בֶּאֱחֹז אֹתוֹ
פְלִשְׁתִּים בְּגַת ׃ 2 חָנֵּנִי אֱלֹהִים כִּי־
שְׁאָפַנִי אֱנוֹשׁ כָּל־הַיּוֹם לֹחֵם
יִלְחָצֵנִי ׃ 3 שָׁאֲפוּ שׁוֹרְרַי כָּל־הַיּוֹם
כִּי־רַבִּים לֹחֲמִים לִי מָרוֹם ׃ 4 יוֹם
אִירָא אֲנִי אֵלֶיךָ אֶבְטָח ׃ 5
בֵּאלֹהִים אֲהַלֵּל דְּבָרוֹ בֵּאלֹהִים
בָּטַחְתִּי לֹא אִירָא מַה־יַּעֲשֶׂה בָשָׂר
לִי ׃ 6 כָּל־הַיּוֹם דְּבָרַי יְעַצֵּבוּ עָלַי
כָּל־מַחְשְׁבֹתָם לָרָע ׃ 7 יָגוּרוּ ׀
יַצְפִּינוּ [וְיִצְפּוֹנוּ] הֵמָּה עֲקֵבַי יִשְׁמֹרוּ
כַּאֲשֶׁר קִוּוּ נַפְשִׁי ׃ 8 עַל־אָוֶן פַּלֶּט־
לָמוֹ בְּאַף עַמִּים ׀ הוֹרֵד אֱלֹהִים ׃ 9
נֹדִי סָפַרְתָּה אָתָּה שִׂימָה דִמְעָתִי
בְנֹאדֶךָ הֲלֹא בְּסִפְרָתֶךָ ׃ 10 אָז
יָשׁוּבוּ אוֹיְבַי אָחוֹר בְּיוֹם אֶקְרָא
זֶה־יָדַעְתִּי כִּי־אֱלֹהִים לִי ׃ 11
בֵּאלֹהִים אֲהַלֵּל דָּבָר בַּיהוָה
אֲהַלֵּל דָּבָר ׃ 12 בֵּאלֹהִים בָּטַחְתִּי
לֹא אִירָא מַה־יַּעֲשֶׂה אָדָם לִי ׃ 13
עָלַי אֱלֹהִים נְדָרֶיךָ אֲשַׁלֵּם תּוֹדֹת
לָךְ ׃ 14 כִּי הִצַּלְתָּ נַפְשִׁי מִמָּוֶת הֲלֹא

Are *they* not in 'Your book?
9 Then my enemies will ^aturn back ^bin the day when I call;
This I know, ¹that 'God is for me.
10 In God, *whose* word I praise,
In the LORD, *whose* word I praise,
11 In God I have put my ¹trust, I shall not be afraid.
What can man do to me?
12 Your ^avows are *binding* upon me, O God;
I will render thank offerings to You.
13 For You have ^adelivered my soul from death,
¹Indeed ^bmy feet from stumbling,
So that I may ^cwalk before God
In the ^dlight of the ²living.

רַגְלִי מִדֶּחִי לְהִתְהַלֵּךְ לִפְנֵי אֱלֹהִים בְּאוֹר הַחַיִּים׃

References

Psalm 56:0
'Or *The silent dove of those who are far off,* or, *The dove of the distant terebinths*
°Possibly *Epigrammatic Poem,* or *Atonement Psalm*
^1 Sam 21:10, 11

Psalm 56:1
¹Or *snapped at*
²Or *A fighting man*
*a*Ps 57:3
*b*Ps 17:9

Psalm 56:2
¹Or *snapped at*
²Or *many are fighting*
*a*Ps 35:25; 57:3; 124:3
*b*Ps 35:1

Psalm 56:3
¹Lit *In the day*
²Or *I am one who puts*
*a*Ps 55:4, 5
*b*Ps 11:1

Psalm 56:4
¹Lit *flesh*
*a*Ps 56:10, 11
*b*Ps 118:6; Heb 13:6

Psalm 56:5
¹Or *trouble my affairs*
²Or *purposes*
*a*2 Pet 3:16
*b*Ps 41:7

Psalm 56:6
¹Or *stir up strife*
²Lit *heels*
³Lit *soul*
*a*Ps 59:3; 140:2; Is 54:15
*b*Ps 17:11

[c]Ps 71:10

Psalm 56:7
[1]Or *will they have escape?*
[a]Ps 36:12; Prov 19:5; Ezek 17:15; Rom 2:3
[b]Ps 55:23

Psalm 56:8
[a]Ps 139:3
[b]2 Kin 20:5; Ps 39:12
[c]Mal 3:16

Psalm 56:9
[1]Or *because*
[a]Ps 9:3
[b]Ps 102:2
[c]Ps 41:11; 118:6; Rom 8:31

Psalm 56:11
[1]Or *trust without fear*

Psalm 56:12
[a]Ps 50:14

Psalm 56:13
[1]Or *have You* not *delivered*
[2]Or *life*
[a]Ps 33:19; 49:15; 86:13
[b]Ps 116:8
[c]Ps 116:9
[d]Job 33:30

Targum

Psa. 56:1 For praise, concerning the congregation of Israel which is likened to a quiet dove when they are far from their cities, yet they repeatedly praise the Lord of the World, like David, humble and innocent, when the Philistines seized him in Gath. ² Have mercy on me, O LORD God, for a sinful man has crushed me beneath him; all the day the foeman will overpower me. ³ My oppressors crush my bones all the day, for many are the oppressors fighting against me, O God Most High, whose throne is on high. ⁴ In the day that I am afraid, I will put my trust in you. ⁵ I will praise the attribute of the justice of God; in the word of God I will put my trust, I will not be afraid. What will flesh do to me? ⁶ All day on my account they toil; against me all their thoughts are for evil. ⁷ They will gather together and they will conceal a trap, they will watch my tracks; as they have waited, they have done to my soul. ⁸ For the lies in their possession, drain them; for the rage of the peoples, make them poor, O God. ⁹ The days of my wandering you have numbered; place my tears in your bottle, O LORD; is not the sum total of my humiliation in your record? ¹⁰ Then my enemies will turn, turning around, on the day that I pray. This I know, for God is my help. ¹¹ In the attribute of justice of God I will give praise in his word; in the attribute of mercy of the LORD I will give praise in his word. ¹² In the word of God I have placed my trust, I will not fear what a son of man will do to me. ¹³ I have taken your vows upon myself, O God; I will repay sacrifices of thanksgiving in your presence. ¹⁴ For you have delivered my soul from being killed, indeed, my feet from bruising, to walk before the LORD in the light of life. [ANOTHER TARGUM: For you have delivered my soul from the death that the sinful die, indeed, my feet from stumbling through sin, so that I will walk before the LORD in the Garden of Eden to behold, the light of the righteous.]

Spiritual Awareness

The spiritual rewrite for the verses is in bold.

In this Psalm, King David exults his miraculous escape from the Philistines. It was a difficult time for David. Saul and his army were chasing him. David decided to enter the territory of the Philistines. He must have thought that the Philistines would protect him; after all, Israel and the Philistines were enemies. However, that is not what happened. David was discovered and dragged to Achish's palace (the king of the Philistines). While he was there, Yishbi, a brother of Goliath, recognized David. Yishbi wanted to kill David as revenge for the death of his brother. Luckily for David, the Shekinah came to him and got him out of the country.

Superscript

The English translation in the NASB 1995 does not translate the full superscript. A possible reason is that Christianity sees the dove as a symbol of the Holy Spirit. This language can be found in the four Gospels of Yeshua's baptism event. However, the dove has not been seen that way by the author of this Psalm. Leviticus 1:14-17 gives a view of the dove in David's day, which is 100% different than the Christian view. The dove is the symbol of a creature that must suffer without being able to defend itself. For David, the helplessness of the dove is equated to his suffering from Saul. David did not have a way to protect himself. Like the dove, he was defenseless and ended up in the land of Israel's enemy.

To the Sefirah Netzach who grants victory, upon the silenced dove who cannot defend itself, of those that are far away. By David; a tenet, when the Philistines took him in Gath.

Verse one

David was convinced at that time that the LORD had some special plan for him. He was anointed to become the king. He had married Saul's daughter. Nevertheless, Saul was trying to kill him. David prays for divine spiritual power and fortitude.

Grant me favor, O God, for Saul pants after me; each day, warlike, he oppresses me.

Verses two, three, four

Some men were filled with rage wanting to kill David. He faced the future unafraid because he trusted in the LORD.

My foes have trampled upon me all day long, for they are many who fight proudly against me.

When I am afraid, I will put my trust in You.

In God, whose word I praise, in God I have put my trust; I shall not be afraid. What can mere man do to me?

Verse five

Saul wants David to utter words of sadness, but he will not.

Every day they would cause my words to be sad; all their thoughts about me are for evil.

Verse six

The men following David were spying on him to find a fault. David believed that his life was an open book because he had nothing to hide (during this time).

They gather together: they lie in wait. They wish to watch my heels even as they hope to find my soul.

Verse seven

If the men following David escape punishment for chasing him, they will be able to use their powers for evil.

Because of wickedness, cast them forth, in anger put down the peoples, O God.

Verse eight

David said that the LORD had counted out the total number of days of his exile. His tears of sadness cannot be stopped. Those tears were for the men who were chasing David. He believed that their actions were treasonous.

You have counted my wanderings in advance. Also, place my tears in Your bottle. Are they not also in Your book?

Verse nine

When the days of suffering appointed to David came to an end, his enemies will be turned back. David believed that the LORD heard his prayers and ended his suffering when this happened.

At the appointed time, my enemies shall turn back on the day on which I call; for this, I know; God is with me.

Verse ten

David accepted the events of his life as events that the LORD ordained.

In God, whose word I praise, in the LORD, whose word I praise

Verse eleven

It was the LORD's nearness that upheld David during these trials.

In God I trust, I know no fear: what can man do unto me?

Verse twelve

David had made pledges to the LORD and wanted to carry them out.

Incumbent upon me, O God, are the vows which I have pledged unto You; I shall render manifold thanks unto You.

Verse thirteen

David acknowledged two aspects of the LORD's aid. First is deliverance from the danger of impending physical annihilation. The second is the spiritual support rendered to his heart.

For even You have delivered my soul from death, have You not also delivered my feet from stumbling? So that, even while He judges me, I may walk before God in the light of life.

Complete Psalm Rewrite Emphasizing Spiritual Awareness

To the Sefirah Netzach who grants victory, upon the silenced dove who cannot defend itself, of those that are far away. By David; a tenet, when the Philistines took him in Gath.

Grant me favor, O God, for Saul pants after me; each day, warlike, he oppresses me.

My foes have trampled upon me all day long, for they are many who fight proudly against me.

When I am afraid, I will put my trust in You.

In God, whose word I praise, in God I have put my trust; I shall not be afraid. What can mere man do to me?

Every day they would cause my words to be sad; all their thoughts about me are for evil.

They gather together: they lie in wait. They wish to watch my heels even as they hope to find my soul.

Because of wickedness, cast them forth, in anger put down the peoples, O God.

You have counted my wanderings in advance. Also, place my tears in Your bottle. Are they not also in Your book?

At the appointed time, my enemies shall turn back on the day on which I call; for this,

I know; God is with me.

In God, whose word I praise, in the LORD, whose word I praise

Psalm 57

New American Standard 1995	Hebrew
Psa. 57:0 For the choir director; *set to* †Al-tashheth. A °Mikhtam of David, ^when he fled from Saul in the cave. **Psa. 57:1** Be gracious to me, O God, be gracious to me, For my soul *a*takes refuge in You; And in the *b*shadow of Your wings I will take refuge Until destruction *c*passes by. 2 I will cry to God Most High, To God who *a*accomplishes *all things* for me. 3 He will *a*send from heaven and save me; He reproaches him who *1b*tramples upon me. *2*Selah. God will send forth His *c*lovingkindness and His *3*truth. **Psa. 57:4** My soul is among *a*lions; I must lie among those who breathe forth fire, *Even* the sons of men, whose *b*teeth are spears and arrows And their *c*tongue a sharp sword. 5 *a*Be exalted above the heavens, O God; *Let* Your glory *be* above all the earth. 6 They have *1*prepared a *a*net for my steps; My soul is *b*bowed down; They *c*dug a pit before me;	לַמְנַצֵּחַ אַל־תַּשְׁחֵת לְדָוִד **Psa. 57:1** מִכְתָּם בְּבָרְחוֹ מִפְּנֵי־שָׁאוּל בַּמְּעָרָה׃ ² חָנֵּנִי אֱלֹהִים וְחָנֵּנִי כִּי בְךָ חָסָיָה נַפְשִׁי וּבְצֵל־כְּנָפֶיךָ אֶחְסֶה עַד יַעֲבֹר הַוּוֹת׃ ³ אֶקְרָא לֵאלֹהִים עֶלְיוֹן לָאֵל גֹּמֵר עָלָי׃ ⁴ יִשְׁלַח מִשָּׁמַיִם וְיוֹשִׁיעֵנִי חֵרֵף שֹׁאֲפִי סֶלָה יִשְׁלַח אֱלֹהִים חַסְדּוֹ וַאֲמִתּוֹ׃ ⁵ נַפְשִׁי בְּתוֹךְ לְבָאִם אֶשְׁכְּבָה לֹהֲטִים בְּנֵי־אָדָם שִׁנֵּיהֶם חֲנִית וְחִצִּים וּלְשׁוֹנָם חֶרֶב חַדָּה׃ ⁶ רוּמָה עַל־הַשָּׁמַיִם אֱלֹהִים עַל כָּל־ הָאָרֶץ כְּבוֹדֶךָ׃ ⁷ רֶשֶׁת וְהֵכִינוּ לִפְעָמַי כָּפַף נַפְשִׁי כָּרוּ לְפָנַי שִׁיחָה נָפְלוּ בְתוֹכָהּ סֶלָה׃ ⁸ נָכוֹן לִבִּי אֱלֹהִים נָכוֹן לִבִּי אָשִׁירָה וַאֲזַמֵּרָה׃ ⁹ עוּרָה כְבוֹדִי עוּרָה הַנֵּבֶל וְכִנּוֹר אָעִירָה שָּׁחַר׃ ¹⁰ אוֹדְךָ בָעַמִּים וְאֲדֹנָי אֲזַמֶּרְךָ בַּל־ אֻמִּים׃ ¹¹ כִּי־גָדֹל עַד־שָׁמַיִם חַסְדֶּךָ וְעַד־שְׁחָקִים אֲמִתֶּךָ׃ ¹² רוּמָה עַל־שָׁמַיִם אֱלֹהִים עַל כָּל־ הָאָרֶץ כְּבוֹדֶךָ׃

They *themselves* have [d]fallen into the midst of it. Selah.

Psa. 57:7   [a]My [b]heart is steadfast, O God, my heart is steadfast;
I will sing, yes, I will sing praises!
8   Awake, [a]my glory!
Awake, [b]harp and lyre!
I will awaken the dawn.
9   [a]I will give thanks to You, O Lord, among the peoples;
I will sing praises to You among the [1]nations.
10   For Your [a]lovingkindness is great to the heavens
And Your [1]truth to the clouds.
11   [a]Be exalted above the heavens, O God;
Let Your glory *be* above all the earth.

References

Psalm 57:0
'Lit *Do Not Destroy*
°Possibly, *Epigrammatic Poem* or *Atonement Psalm*
^1 Sam 22:1; 24:3

Psalm 57:1
*a*Ps 2:12; 34:22
*b*Ruth 2:12; Ps 17:8; 36:7; 63:7; 91:4
*c*Is 26:20

Psalm 57:2
*a*Ps 138:8

Psalm 57:3
1Or *snaps at*
2*Selah* may mean: *Pause, Crescendo* or *Musical interlude*
3Or *faithfulness*
*a*Ps 18:16; 144:5, 7
*b*Ps 56:2
*c*Ps 25:10; 40:11

Psalm 57:4
*a*Ps 35:17; 58:6
*b*Prov 30:14
*c*Ps 55:21; 59:7; 64:3; Prov 12:18

Psalm 57:5
*a*Ps 57:11; 108:5

Psalm 57:6
1Or *spread*
*a*Ps 10:9; 31:4; 35:7; 140:5
*b*Ps 145:14
*c*Ps 7:15
*d*Prov 26:27; 28:10; Eccl 10:8

Psalm 57:7
*a*Ps 57:7-11; 108:1-5
*b*Ps 112:7

Psalm 57:8
[a]Ps 16:9; 30:12
[b]Ps 150:3

Psalm 57:9
[1]Lit *peoples*
[a]Ps 108:3

Psalm 57:10
[1]Or *faithfulness*
[a]Ps 36:5; 103:11; 108:4

Psalm 57:11
[a]Ps 57:5; 108:5

Targum

Psa. 57:1 For praise, concerning the distress at the time when David said, "Do not harm." It was spoken by David, humble and innocent, when he fled from Saul's presence in the cave. ² Have mercy on me, O God, have mercy on me, for in your word my soul has trusted, and in the shade of your Presence I will be confident until the turmoil passes. ³ I will pray before God Most High, the mighty one, who commanded the spider who completed a web for me. ⁴ He will send his angel from heaven above, and he will redeem me; he has put to shame the one who bruises me, forever; God will send his goodness and his truth. ⁵ My soul glows while in the midst of flames; I will sleep among coals that burn, the sons of men whose teeth are like lances and arrows, and whose tongue is like a sharp sword. ⁶ Be exalted over the angels of heaven, O God; your glory is over all those who dwell on earth. ⁷ They have set a net for my footsteps; my soul is bowed down; they dug before me a pit, they have fallen into the middle of it forever. ⁸ My heart is turned to your Torah, O LORD; my heart is turned to fear you; I will praise and sing! ⁹ Wake up, my glory! Wake up to praise by means of the harp and lyre; wake up for the prayer of morning. ¹⁰ I will give thanks before you among the peoples, O LORD; I will praise you among the nations. ¹¹ For your goodness is high to reach the heavens, and your truth, to the clouds. ¹² Be exalted, O LORD, above the angels of heaven; O God, above all the inhabitants of the earth is your glory.

Spiritual Awareness

The spiritual rewrite for the verses is in bold.

Introduction

King Saul and three thousand of his soldiers were chasing David through the wilderness of En-Gedi. Saul walked into a cave where David and his men were hiding. While Saul was relieving himself, David's men wanted to kill him. Instead, David decided to cut off a piece of Saul's cloak, thus proving David's loyalty to Saul. David hoped that Saul would stop pursuing him in order to kill him.

אַל־תַּשְׁחֵת (al – tash'chat) means "not destroy." This phrase is found in the superscript of Psalms 57, 58, 59, and 75. All four psalms deal with conditions of potential general ruin and corruption unless the LORD would intervene and put a stop to it.

To the Sefirah Netzach who grants victory. Let not destruction come. A psalm by David when he fled from Saul in the cave.

Verse one

David was placed under a tremendous test of moral and spiritual fortitude. He needed a divine factor to make the godly choice.

Endow my spirit O God, endow my spirit, for in You my soul puts its trust. And I shall trustingly hide myself in the shadow of Your wings until that which is now being shaped shall have passed.

Verse two

Even though the LORD seems far away from David, he calls upon Him for help.

I will call upon God, the Most High, to the Almighty one who decrees my fate.

Verse three

Saul and his men were chasing an innocent David. Since they wanted to kill him and he was the anointed one of the LORD, these men were blasphemers.

He will send from heaven and save me; He reproaches him who tramples upon me. Meditate on this verse. God will send forth His lovingkindness and His truth.

Verse four

David uses the metaphor of the lion to refer to the men pursuing him. When a lion kills, it is not concerned about the animal it kills. To lie down with the lions means that David was confident that Saul's men would not kill him because the LORD was protecting him.

As for me, amidst lions, I lie down peacefully beside those aflame with rage, sons of man whose teeth are spears and arrows and whose tongue is a sharp sword.

Verse five

Even though the LORD is in the Heavens, His glory is felt and seen upon the earth.

Yet even though You are high above the heavens, Your glory is upon the earth.

Verse six

David says that Saul's men had tried to kill him before. However, the LORD helped David.

They have prepared a net for my steps; My soul is bowed down; They dug a pit before me; They have fallen into the midst of it. Meditate on this verse.

Verse seven

David's enemies had hoped to change David's heart. However, they succeeded in strengthening David's reliance on the LORD. The repetition is for emphasis.

My heart was made steadfast, O God, my heart was made steadfast, so that I uttered hymns and sang songs.

Verse eight

The individual must do spiritual growth and awakening. Repetition is used for emphasis.

Awake, O my honor, awake, O psaltery and harp; I shall awaken the dawn.

Verse nine

David was in flight, persecuted, and hiding in a dark cave. Things looked bad for David. However, he praised the LORD.

I will acknowledge You among the peoples, my Master, I will sing praises unto You among the nations.

Verse ten

The Sefirah Chesed is great in Heaven and Your faithfulness unto the clouds.

Verse Eleven

Yet even though You are High above heavens, Your glory is upon all the earth.

Complete Psalm Rewrite Emphasizing Spiritual Awareness

To the Sefirah Netzach who grants victory. Let not destruction come. A psalm by David when he fled from Saul in the cave.

Endow my spirit O God, endow my spirit, for in You my soul puts its trust. And I shall trustingly hide myself in the shadow of Your wings until that which is now being shaped shall have passed.

I will call upon God, the Most High, to the Almighty one who decrees my fate.

He will send from heaven and save me; He reproaches him who tramples upon me. Meditate on this verse. God will send forth His lovingkindness and His truth.

As for me, amidst lions, I lie down peacefully beside those aflame with rage, sons of man whose teeth are spears and arrows and whose tongue is a sharp sword.

Yet even though You are high above the heavens, Your glory is upon the earth.

They have prepared a net for my steps; My soul is bowed down; They dug a pit before me; They have fallen into the midst of it. Meditate on this verse.

My heart was made steadfast, O God, my heart was made steadfast, so that I uttered hymns and sang songs.

Awake, O my honor, awake, O psaltery and harp; I shall awaken the dawn.

I will acknowledge You among the peoples, my Master, I will sing praises unto You among the nations.

The Sefirah Chesed is great in Heaven and Your faithfulness unto the clouds.

Yet even though You are High above heavens, Your glory is upon all the earth.

Psalm 58

New American Standard 1995	Hebrew

Psa. 58:0 For the choir director; *set to* †Al-tashheth. A °Mikhtam of David.

Psa. 58:1 Do you indeed [1]speak righteousness, O [2]gods?
Do you [a]judge [3]uprightly, O sons of men?
[2] No, in heart you [a]work unrighteousness;
On earth you [b]weigh out the violence of your hands.
[3] The wicked are estranged [a]from the womb;
These who speak lies [b]go astray from [1]birth.
[4] They have venom like the [a]venom of a serpent;
Like a deaf cobra that stops up its ear,
[5] So that it [a]does not hear the voice of [1b]charmers,
Or a skillful caster of spells.

Psa. 58:6 O God, [a]shatter their teeth in their mouth;
Break out the fangs of the young lions, O LORD.
[7] Let them [a]flow away like water that runs off;
When he [1b]aims his arrows, let them be as [2]headless shafts.
[8] *Let them be* as a snail which [1]melts away as it goes along,
Like the [a]miscarriages of a woman which never see the sun.

לַֽמְנַצֵּחַ אַל־תַּשְׁחֵת **Psa. 58:1**
לְדָוִד מִכְתָּם : [2] הַֽאֻמְנָם
אֵלֶם צֶדֶק תְּדַבֵּרוּן מֵישָׁרִים
תִּשְׁפְּטוּ בְּנֵי אָדָם : [3] אַף־
בְּלֵב עוֹלֹת תִּפְעָלוּן בָּאָרֶץ
חֲמַס יְדֵיכֶם תְּפַלֵּסוּן : [4] זֹרוּ
רְשָׁעִים מֵרָחֶם תָּעוּ מִבֶּטֶן
דֹּבְרֵי כָזָב : [5] חֲמַת־לָמוֹ
כִּדְמוּת חֲמַת־נָחָשׁ כְּמוֹ־פֶתֶן
חֵרֵשׁ יַאְטֵם אָזְנוֹ : [6] אֲשֶׁר
לֹא־יִשְׁמַע לְקוֹל מְלַחֲשִׁים
חוֹבֵר חֲבָרִים מְחֻכָּם : [7]
אֱלֹהִים הֲרָס־שִׁנֵּימוֹ בְּפִימוֹ
מַלְתְּעוֹת כְּפִירִים נְתֹץ |
יְהוָה : [8] יִמָּאֲסוּ כְמוֹ־מַיִם
יִתְהַלְּכוּ־לָמוֹ יִדְרֹךְ חִצָּו
[חִצָּיו] כְּמוֹ יִתְמֹלָלוּ : [9] כְּמוֹ
שַׁבְּלוּל תֶּמֶס יַהֲלֹךְ נֵפֶל
אֵשֶׁת בַּל־חָזוּ שָׁמֶשׁ : [10]

<table>
<tr><td>

9 Before your ^apots can feel *the fire of* thorns

He will ^bsweep them away with a whirlwind, the ¹green and the burning alike.

Psa. 58:10 The ^arighteous will rejoice when he ^bsees the vengeance;

He will ^cwash his feet in the blood of the wicked.

11 And men will say, "Surely there is a ^{1a}reward for the righteous;

Surely there is a God who ^bjudges ²on earth!"

</td><td dir="rtl">

בְּטֶרֶם יָבִינוּ סִּירֹתֵיכֶם אָטָד כְּמוֹ־חַי כְּמוֹ־חָרוֹן יִשְׂעָרֶנּוּ:

11 יִשְׂמַח צַדִּיק כִּי־חָזָה נָקָם פְּעָמָיו יִרְחַץ בְּדַם הָרָשָׁע:

12 וְיֹאמַר אָדָם אַךְ־פְּרִי לַצַּדִּיק אַךְ יֵשׁ־אֱלֹהִים שֹׁפְטִים בָּאָרֶץ:

</td></tr>
</table>

References

Psalm 57:0
†Lit *Do Not Destroy*
°Possibly, *Epigrammatic Poem* or *Atonement Psalm*
^1 Sam 22:1; 24:3

Psalm 57:1
*a*Ps 2:12; 34:22
*b*Ruth 2:12; Ps 17:8; 36:7; 63:7; 91:4
*c*Is 26:20

Psalm 57:2
*a*Ps 138:8

Psalm 57:3
¹Or *snaps at*
²*Selah* may mean: *Pause, Crescendo* or *Musical interlude*
³Or *faithfulness*
*a*Ps 18:16; 144:5, 7
*b*Ps 56:2
*c*Ps 25:10; 40:11

Psalm 57:4
*a*Ps 35:17; 58:6
*b*Prov 30:14
*c*Ps 55:21; 59:7; 64:3; Prov 12:18

Psalm 57:5
*a*Ps 57:11; 108:5

Psalm 57:6
¹Or *spread*
*a*Ps 10:9; 31:4; 35:7; 140:5
*b*Ps 145:14
*c*Ps 7:15
*d*Prov 26:27; 28:10; Eccl 10:8

Psalm 57:7
*a*Ps 57:7-11; 108:1-5
*b*Ps 112:7

Psalm 57:8
[a]Ps 16:9; 30:12
[b]Ps 150:3

Psalm 57:9
[1]Lit *peoples*
[a]Ps 108:3

Psalm 57:10
[1]Or *faithfulness*
[a]Ps 36:5; 103:11; 108:4

Psalm 57:11
[a]Ps 57:5; 108:5

Targum

Psa. 58:1 For praise; concerning the distress in the time when David said, "Do no harm"; composed by David, humble and innocent. [2] In very truth are you silent, O righteous ones, in the time of strife? It is fitting that you speak righteousness, that you judge uprightly the sons of men. [3] But, O wicked, wherefore do you commit iniquity in the heart, wherefore do your hands establish crime on the earth? [4] The wicked have become strangers from birth; those who utter falsehood have gone astray from the womb. [5] Poison is theirs like the poison of the serpent; like the deaf adder that stops up his ears. [6] Lest it should accept the words of the wizards, the charmers of snakes; he is wiser than those who cast spells. [7] O God, smash their teeth in their mouth; and shatter the fangs of the lions' offspring, O LORD. [8] Let them dissolve in their sins; like water, let them flow away; and he draws arrows at them, and they will be cut in pieces. [9] Like the crawling snail whose path is disgusting, like the abortion and the mole who are blind and have not seen the sun; [10] Before the soft wicked become as hard as thorns, while they are moist, while they are like unripe fruit, may he destroy them by the storm wind. [11] The righteous will rejoice, for he has seen retribution on them; he will wash his feet in the blood of the wicked man. [12] And the sons of men will say, "Truly, there is a good reward for the righteous, truly there is a God whose judgments extend to the earth."

Spiritual Awareness

The spiritual rewrite for the verses is in bold.

Introduction and Superscript

In the previous Psalm, David did not allow his men to kill Saul when he entered the cave they were hiding in. David allowed Saul to live and cut off a piece of his cloak. David hoped that this demonstrated to Saul his loyalty. This Psalm talks about Saul's underlings who conspired to destroy David's goodwill.

Midrash Shocher Tov says that Saul's underlings came to him and argued that David was not a righteous man. If David had killed Saul in the cave, David knew he would have been torn limb by limb.

Talmud tractate Yerushalmi Sotah 1:8 says that Saul's leading general, Abner claimed that Saul's garment tore on a thorn, and David recovered the piece of apparel and was using it to trick Saul.

To the Sefirah Netzach who grants victory. Let not destruction come. A tenet by David.

Verse one

הַאֻמְנָם (haoom'nam) – means "indeed." This word can also mean "in truth."

When the הַ is added, it becomes a question, "Is it true?" or "Is it truly so?"

תִּשְׁפְּטוּ (teesh'p'tu) – means "to judge." This word does not necessarily mean legal enforcement of justice based on a witness. Instead, it is used to indicate a social judgment.

Is silence truly just when you should speak instead? When should you judge the sons of man in equity?

Verse two

What constrains a person from speaking the truth against lawlessness?

Even with your hearts, you commit atrocities. You weigh out the wrong of your hands in the land.

Verses three, four, and five

The preceding verses were a reproach to those who could have acted to put a stop to evil. David charges them with being accomplices in the wrong that has been perpetrated because they have failed to teach, warn, or remonstrate with sinners.

And if the lawless are estranged [from good] from the mother's womb, if liars go astray from birth.

If their raging is like the rage of a serpent, like a deaf viper which closes its ear,

Which does not harken to the voice of the charmers, of the most cunning binder of spells.

Verse six

David calls upon all qualified men to wield their power to prevent evil. There were no men available.

Then you are in God's place! Break their teeth in their mouths; to destroy the teeth of lions is the work of the LORD with loving kindness.

Verse seven

Society makes itself an accomplice to all evil in this world as long as it accepts crime. Also, society's acceptance of all immorality will bring its downfall. This is seen today when woke District Attorneys blame victims for perpetrators' crimes. Today's society has decided to consider a lot of the immorality of the woke crowd acceptable. This can become society's downfall.

Despised, they would melt away like water; they would steal away even if one of them aims his arrows; it is as though they crumbled away.

Verse eight

The next verses are the finishing remarks of the description of the gradual disappearance of evil that would be brought about by the intervention of righteous people. Unfortunately, in today's society, the woke are excellent trolls. They know how to attack anyone who opposes their immoral changes to society. This creates the silent majority who will have to one day rise up against evil. When David was being chased by Saul, many people wanted to stand for David but knew they would be executed by Saul. Therefore, they did not come forward until Saul's death.

Even as the snail which melts and slithers away, as the stillbirth of a woman, both of which have never seen the sun.

Verse nine

Rabbi Hirsch said that this is a difficult verse to interpret. He offered that we need to muster all the forces of good for the intervention against evil. Evil in Saul's day was intense and shown through Saul's madness to kill David. David was loyal to Saul and was his son-in-law. That did not stop evil from conquering Saul. It is going to take all of the goodness of the world to stop the evil that has taken over.

Before your thinner thorns can reveal the brier as if it were alive, as if evil incarnate is sweeping one away with a whirlwind.

Verse ten

The word "blood" in this verse denotes the vengeance that was threatening wicked people. There is no call for killing in the Psalm. Therefore, blood denotes vengeance. David tells the righteous that they must drive away the wicked. The righteous traits will help other people resolve their lives and make themselves pure. Evil people can be turned by the acts and words of the righteous.

But the righteous person shall rejoice when they foresee vengeance; they shall keep their own steps all the more pursed at the time of the destruction of the wicked.

Verse eleven

Righteousness can offer a reward on Earth or later in Heaven.

And men shall say, "Indeed there is still a reward for the righteous; there are still those who act in God's place, as judges in the land."

Complete Psalm Rewrite Emphasizing Spiritual Awareness

To the Sefirah Netzach who grants victory. Let not destruction come. A tenet by David.

Is silence truly just when you should speak instead? When should you judge the sons of man in equity?

Even with your hearts, you commit atrocities. You weigh out the wrong of your hands in the land.

And if the lawless are estranged [from good] from the mother's womb, if liars go astray from birth.

If their raging is like the rage of a serpent, like a deaf viper which closes its ear,

Which does not harken to the voice of the charmers, of the most cunning binder of spells.

Then you are in God's place! Break their teeth in their mouths; to destroy the teeth of lions is the work of the LORD with loving kindness.

Despised, they would melt away like water; they would steal away even if one of them aims his arrows; it is as though they crumbled away.

Even as the snail which melts and slithers away, as the stillbirth of a woman, both of which have never seen the sun.

Before your thinner thorns can reveal the brier as if it were alive, as if evil incarnate is sweeping one away with a whirlwind.

But the righteous person shall rejoice when they foresee vengeance; they shall keep their own steps all the more pursed at the time of the destruction of the wicked.

And men shall say, "Indeed there is still a reward for the righteous; there are still those who act in God's place, as judges in the land."

Psalm 59

New American Standard 1995	Hebrew

Psa. 59:0 For the choir director; *set to* †Al-tashheth. A °Mikhtam of David, ˆwhen Saul sent *men* and they watched the house in order to kill him.

Psa. 59:1 ᵃDeliver me from my enemies, O my God;

¹ᵇSet me *securely* on high away from those who rise up against me.

2 Deliver me from ᵃthose who do iniquity

And save me from ᵇmen of bloodshed.

3 For behold, they ᵃhave ¹set an ambush for my ²life;

³Fierce men ⁴ᵃlaunch an attack against me,

ᵇNot for my transgression nor for my sin, O LORD,

4 ¹ᵃFor no guilt of *mine,* they run and set themselves against me.

ᵇArouse Yourself to ²help me, and see!

5 You, ᵃO LORD God of hosts, the God of Israel,

Awake to ¹ᵇpunish all the nations;

ᶜDo not be gracious to any *who are* treacherous in iniquity.   ²Selah.

6 They ᵃreturn at evening, they howl like a ᵇdog,

And go around the city.

7 Behold, they ᵃbelch forth with their mouth;

ᵇSwords are in their lips,

For, *they say,* "ᶜWho hears?"

Psa. 59:1 לַמְנַצֵּחַ אַל־תַּשְׁחֵת֘ לְדָוִ֪ד מִ֫כְתָּ֥ם בִּשְׁלֹ֥חַ שָׁא֑וּל וַֽיִּשְׁמְרוּ֙ אֶת־הַבַּ֔יִת לַהֲמִיתֽוֹ׃ 2 הַצִּילֵ֖נִי מֵאֹיְבַ֥י ׀ אֱלֹהָ֑י מִֽמִּתְקוֹמְמַ֥י תְּשַׂגְּבֵֽנִי׃ 3 הַצִּילֵנִי מִפֹּ֣עֲלֵי אָ֑וֶן וּֽמֵאַנְשֵׁ֥י דָ֝מִ֗ים הוֹשִׁיעֵֽנִי׃ 4 כִּ֤י הִנֵּ֪ה אָֽרְב֡וּ לְנַפְשִׁי֮ יָג֤וּרוּ עָלַ֬י עַזִ֑ים לֹא־פִשְׁעִ֖י וְלֹא־חַטָּאתִ֣י יְהוָֽה׃ 5 בְּֽלִי־עָ֭וֹן יְרוּצ֣וּן וְיִכּוֹנָ֑נוּ ע֖וּרָה לִקְרָאתִ֣י וּרְאֵֽה׃ 6 וְאַתָּ֤ה יְהוָֽה־אֱלֹהִ֥ים ׀ צְבָא֡וֹת אֱלֹ֘הֵ֤י יִשְׂרָאֵ֗ל הָקִ֗יצָה לִפְקֹ֥ד כָּֽל־הַגּוֹיִ֑ם אַל־תָּחֹ֨ן כָּל־בֹּ֖גְדֵי אָ֣וֶן סֶֽלָה׃ 7 יָשׁ֣וּבוּ לָעֶ֑רֶב יֶהֱמ֥וּ כַכָּ֗לֶב וִיס֥וֹבְבוּ עִֽיר׃ 8 הִנֵּ֤ה ׀ יַבִּ֬יעוּן בְּפִיהֶ֗ם חֲ֭רָבוֹת בְּשִׂפְתוֹתֵיהֶ֑ם כִּי־מִ֥י שֹׁמֵֽעַ׃ 9 וְאַתָּ֣ה יְ֭הוָה תִּשְׂחַק־לָ֑מוֹ תִּ֝לְעַ֗ג לְכָל־גּוֹיִֽם׃ 10 עֻ֭זּוֹ אֵלֶ֣יךָ אֶשְׁמֹ֑רָה כִּֽי־אֱ֝לֹהִ֗ים מִשְׂגַּבִּֽי׃ 11 אֱלֹהֵ֣י חַסְדּ֣וֹ [חַסְדִּ֣י] יְקַדְּמֵ֑נִי אֱ֝לֹהִ֗ים יַרְאֵ֥נִי בְשֹׁרְרָֽי׃ 12 אַל־תַּהַרְגֵ֤ם ׀ פֶּֽן־יִשְׁכְּח֬וּ עַמִּ֗י הֲנִיעֵ֣מוֹ בְחֵ֭ילְךָ וְהוֹרִידֵ֑מוֹ מָֽגִנֵּ֣נוּ אֲדֹנָֽי׃ 13 חַטַּאת־פִּ֗ימוֹ דְּֽבַר־שְׂפָ֫תֵ֥ימוֹ וְיִלָּכְד֥וּ בִגְאוֹנָ֑ם וּמֵאָלָ֖ה וּמִכַּ֣חַשׁ יְסַפֵּֽרוּ׃ 14 כַּלֵּ֥ה בְחֵמָה֮ כַּלֵּ֤ה

8 But You, O LORD, *a*laugh at them;

You *b*scoff at all the nations.

Psa. 59:9 *Because of* [1]his *a*strength I will watch for You,

For God is my *b*stronghold.

10 [1]My God *a*in His lovingkindness will meet me;

God will let me *b*look *triumphantly* upon [2]my foes.

11 Do not slay them, *a*or my people will forget;

[1b]Scatter them by Your power, and bring them down,

O Lord, *c*our shield.

12 [1]*On account of* the *a*sin of their mouth *and* the words of their lips,

Let them even be *b*caught in their pride,

And on account of *c*curses and [2]lies which they utter.

13 [1a]Destroy *them* in wrath, [1]destroy *them* that they may be no more;

That *men* may *b*know that God [2]rules in Jacob

To the ends of the earth. Selah.

14 They *a*return at evening, they howl like a dog,

And go around the city.

15 They *a*wander about [1]for food

And [2]growl if they are not satisfied.

Psa. 59:16 But as for me, I shall *a*sing of Your strength;

Yes, I shall *b*joyfully sing of Your lovingkindness in the *c*morning,

For You have been my *d*stronghold

And a *e*refuge in the day of my distress.

וְֽאִינֵ֥מוֹ וְֽיֵדְע֗וּ כִּֽי־אֱ֭לֹהִים מֹשֵׁ֣ל
15 בְּֽיַעֲקֹ֑ב לְאַפְסֵ֖י הָאָ֣רֶץ סֶֽלָה׃
וְיָשׁ֣וּבוּ לָ֭עֶרֶב יֶהֱמ֥וּ כַכָּ֗לֶב וִיס֥וֹבְבוּ
16 עִֽיר׃ הֵ֭מָּה יְנוּע֣וּן [יְנִיע֣וּן]
17 לֶאֱכֹ֑ל אִם־לֹ֥א יִ֝שְׂבְּע֗וּ וַיָּלִֽינוּ׃
וַאֲנִ֤י ׀ אָשִׁ֣יר עֻזֶּךָ֮ וַאֲרַנֵּ֥ן לַבֹּ֗קֶר
חַ֫סְדֶּ֥ךָ כִּֽי־הָיִ֣יתָ מִשְׂגָּ֣ב לִ֑י וּ֝מָנ֗וֹס
18 בְּי֣וֹם צַר־לִֽי׃ עֻ֭זִּי אֵלֶ֣יךָ אֲזַמֵּ֑רָה
כִּֽי־אֱלֹהִ֥ים מִ֝שְׂגַּבִּ֗י אֱלֹהֵ֥י חַסְדִּֽי׃

17 [a]O my strength, I will sing praises to You; For God is my [b]stronghold, the [1]God who shows me lovingkindness.	

References

Psalm 59:0
†Lit *Do Not Destroy*
°Possibly *Epigrammatic Poem* or *Atonement Psalm*
^1 Sam 19:11

Psalm 59:1
[1]Or *May You put me in an inaccessibly high place*
[a]Ps 143:9
[b]Ps 20:1; 69:29

Psalm 59:2
[a]Ps 28:3; 36:12; 53:4; 92:7; 94:16
[b]Ps 26:9; 139:19; Prov 29:10

Psalm 59:3
[1]Or *lain in wait*
[2]Lit *soul*
[3]Or *Strong*
[4]Or *stir up strife*
[a]Ps 56:6
[b]1 Sam 24:11; Ps 7:3, 4; 69:4

Psalm 59:4
[1]Lit *Without guilt*
[2]Lit *meet*
[a]Ps 35:19
[b]Ps 7:6; 35:23

Psalm 59:5
[1]Lit *visit*
[2]*Selah* may mean: *Pause, Crescendo* or *Musical interlude*
[a]Ps 69:6; 80:4; 84:8
[b]Ps 9:5; Is 26:14
[c]Is 2:9; Jer 18:23

Psalm 59:6
[a]Ps 59:14
[b]Ps 22:16

Psalm 59:7
[a]Ps 94:4; Prov 15:2, 28
[b]Ps 57:4; Prov 12:18
[c]Job 22:13; Ps 10:11; 73:11; 94:7

Psalm 59:8
[a]Ps 37:13; Prov 1:26
[b]Ps 2:4

Psalm 59:9
[1]Many mss and some ancient versions read *My strength*
[a]Ps 18:17
[b]Ps 9:9; 62:2

Psalm 59:10
[1]Many mss and some ancient versions read *The God of my lovingkindness*
[2]Lit *those who lie in wait for me*
[a]Ps 21:3
[b]Ps 54:7

Psalm 59:11
[1]Or *Make them wander*
[a]Deut 4:9; 6:12
[b]Ps 106:27; 144:6; Is 33:3
[c]Ps 84:9

Psalm 59:12
[1]Or *The sin of their mouth is the word of their lips,*
[2]Lit *lying*
[a]Prov 12:13
[b]Zeph 3:11
[c]Ps 10:7

Psalm 59:13
[1]Lit *Bring to an end*
[2]Or *is Ruler*
[a]Ps 104:35
[b]Ps 83:18

Psalm 59:14
[a]Ps 59:6

Psalm 59:15

[1]Or *to devour*
[2]Another reading is *tarry all night*
[a]Job 15:23

Psalm 59:16

[a]Ps 21:13
[b]Ps 101:1
[c]Ps 5:3; 88:13
[d]Ps 59:9
[e]2 Sam 22:3; Ps 46:1

Psalm 59:17

[1]Lit *God of my lovingkindness*
[a]Ps 59:9
[b]Ps 59:10

Targum

Psa. 59:1 For praise; concerning the distress when David said, "Do no harm"; composed by David, humble and innocent; when Saul sent and they guarded the house in order to kill him. **2** Deliver me from my enemies, O God; from those who rise against me, save me. **3** Deliver me from those who practice deceit, and from murderous men redeem me. **4** For behold, they have lain in wait for my soul, the strong gathering against me; not on account of my iniquity, and not on account of my sin, O LORD. **5** Before [there are] iniquities, they run and prepare battle; be strong towards me, and see! **6** But you, O LORD God Sabaoth, God of Israel, awake to punish all the Gentiles; do not pity any of the deceitful rulers forever. **7** They will return at evening, they will raise a tumult like a dog, and they will encircle the city. **8** Behold, they will spew forth with their mouth words sharp as swords; with their lips they say, "Let us boast, for who is the one who will hear and punish?" **9** But you, O LORD, will laugh at them; you will mock all the Gentiles. **10** O my strength, for you I will keep watch, for God is my deliverance. **11** God will precede me with my favor, God will show me vengeance on my oppressors. **12** Do not kill them immediately, lest my people forget; exile them from their houses by your might, and impoverish them from their wealth, our shield, O LORD. **13** Because of the sin of their mouth, and the speech of their lips, let them be caught in their arrogance, for they will speak with oaths and lies. **14** Destroy them in anger, destroy them until they are no more, that they may know that God rules in Jacob to the ends of the earth forever. **15** And they will return at evening, they will raise a tumult like a dog, and they will encircle the city. **16** They will wander about to take spoil to eat, and they will not rest until they are full and take lodging. **17** But I will praise your strength, and I rejoice in your goodness in the morning, for you have been a deliverer to me, and my trust in the day I am distressed. **18** O my strength, I will give you praise, for God is my deliverance, God is my goodness.

Spiritual Awareness

The spiritual rewrite for the verses is in bold.

Introduction

David was on the rise, gaining ascendancy, while Saul sank into the lowest depths. David played music for Saul to soothe his anguish until one day, Saul got angry and threw a spear at David's head, barely missing him. At that point, David fled the palace. David's wife was Michal, who was Saul's daughter. She favored David over her father and helped David to escape through a side window. As a ruse, Michal placed a lifelike mannequin (probably a teraphim angel) in David's bed. When Saul demanded that David be brought before him, Michal claimed he was ill and could not get out of bed. Saul dispatched messengers, saying, "Bring him back to me in his bed so that I myself can slay him." When the soldiers went with the messengers to collect David, they discovered they were deceived. David was gone.

David composed this Psalm of entreaty and thanksgiving upon his narrow escape from Saul.

The superscript offers the theme of this Psalm. Saul was raging with jealousy. Saul did not want David killed in his own home because his wife was Saul's daughter. That is why Saul demanded that David be brought before him.

To the Sefirah Netzach who offers victory. Let not destruction come. A tenet by David when Saul sent soldiers to watch the house in order to slay him.

Verse one

The real source of danger for the kingdom was Saul. In this Psalm, David only speaks about the men who, instead of appeasing Saul's insane jealousy of David, did everything they could to fan Saul's hostility even more. They became the tools of Saul's plot against David.

Deliver me from my enemies, O God. Set me up on high over those who rise up against me.

Verse two

The soldiers who were trying to carry out Saul's orders were workers of violence.

Deliver me from the workers of violence and save me from blood-thirsty men.

Verses three and four

David said the soldiers looking for him became strong because they worked together for a common goal. They wanted to bring David back to Saul not because of David's sins but of some other situation.

For behold, they lie in wait for my soul, impudently they gather together against me; it is not for my transgressions and not for my sins, O merciful LORD.

It is not because of my faults that they run and prepare themselves; awake to help me and behold.

Verse five

David asked the LORD why men of violence are allowed to exist, especially in Israel

And you, O LORD, God of Hosts, the God of Israel, arouse Yourself to remember all the nations; show not favor to all the faithless men of violence. Meditate on this verse.

Verse six

They return toward evening; they howl like dogs and go around the city.

Verse seven

The men chasing David were open about their intentions. Their words were more deadly than their swords.

Behold, they spew forth everything from their mouths, swords are in their lips, for "Who hears it?"

Verse eight

The LORD sends suffering to innocent men to test and train them. A righteous man will never be allowed to perish. David saw this part of his life as a test and for training that would enable him to become the king of Israel.

However, You are the LORD. You shall laugh at them. You mock all the nations.

Verse nine

David said to the LORD that as long as Saul held onto the monarchy's power, he would wait until it was his turn. This demonstrated David's love and trust in the LORD.

So long as Saul is in power, I will wait. I will trust you, LORD.

Verse ten

David felt that the LORD would reveal the Sefirah Chesed (mercy, love, lovingkindness) to him.

LORD, please allow me to feel the power of the Sefirah Chesed.

Verse eleven

David did not want the people to forget what Saul did against him.

Slay them not, lest my people forget it; stagger them to your might and cast them down from their high places. O our shield, my Master.

Verse twelve

Every word from the violent men constitutes a misuse of the gift of speech. David asked the LORD to let their arrogance bring about their downfall.

The word of their lips is a sinful use of their mouth, so may they become entangled in their pride and tell of perjury and falsehood.

Verse thirteen

God's people are called Jacob and not Israel. This indicates that the Jewish people are not worthy of the name Israel as long as it will not use its God-given power in His service and the cause of justice and truth.

Let them vanish in wrath, let them vanish until they shall be no more, and then one will know unto the ends of the earth that the LORD rules in Jacob. Meditate on this verse.

Verses fourteen and fifteen

In David's day, dogs howled at night while finding food. The men tracking David were howling for revenge.

They return toward evening; they howl like dogs and go around the city.

They cause commotion in order to eat if they have not had their fill at the place where they have lodged for the night.

Verse sixteen

But as for me, I shall sing of Your all-conquering might, and rejoice in Your mercy toward the morning, how You have been my high tower and a refuge on the day on which I was distressed.

Verse seventeen

Once the power shall be mine, I shall sing praises to You, for God is my high tower, the God of my devotion.

Complete Psalm Rewrite Emphasizing Spiritual Awareness

Deliver me from my enemies, O God. Set me up on high over those who rise up against me.

Deliver me from the workers of violence and save me from blood-thirsty men.

For behold, they lie in wait for my soul, impudently they gather together against me; it is not for my transgressions and not for my sins, O merciful LORD.

It is not because of my faults that they run and prepare themselves; awake to help me and behold.

And you, O LORD, God of Hosts, the God of Israel, arouse Yourself to remember all the nations; show not favor to all the faithless men of violence. Meditate on this verse.

They return toward evening; they howl like dogs and go around the city.

Behold, they spew forth everything from their mouths, swords are in their lips, for "Who hears it?"

However, You are the LORD. You shall laugh at them. You mock all the nations.

So long as Saul is in power, I will wait. I will trust you, LORD.

LORD, please allow me to feel the power of the Sefirah Chesed.

Slay them not, lest my people forget it; stagger them to your might and cast them down from their high places. O our shield, my Master.

The word of their lips is a sinful use of their mouth, so may they become entangled in their pride and tell of perjury and falsehood.

Let them vanish in wrath, let them vanish until they shall be no more, and then one will know unto the ends of the earth that the LORD rules in Jacob. Meditate on this verse.

They return toward evening; they howl like dogs and go around the city.

They cause commotion in order to eat if they have not had their fill at the place where they have lodged for the night.

But as for me, I shall sing of Your all-conquering might, and rejoice in Your mercy toward the morning, how You have been my high tower and a refuge on the day on which I was distressed.

Once the power shall be mine, I shall sing praises to You, for God is my high tower, the God of my devotion.

Psalm 60

New American Standard 1995	Hebrew

Psa. 60:0 For the choir director; according to ʼShushan Eduth. A °Mikhtam of David, to teach; ^when he struggled with Aram-naharaim and with Aram-zobah, and Joab returned, and smote twelve thousand of Edom in the Valley of Salt.

Psa. 60:1 O God, [a]You have rejected us. You have [1b]broken us;

You have been [c]angry; O, [d]restore us.

[2] You have made the [1a]land quake, You have split it open;

[b]Heal its breaches, for it totters.

[3] You have [1a]made Your people experience hardship;

You have given us [2]wine to [b]drink that makes us stagger.

[4] You have given a [a]banner to those who fear You,

That it may be displayed because of the truth. [1]Selah.

[5] [a]That Your [b]beloved may be delivered,

[c]Save with Your right hand, and answer [1]us!

Psa. 60:6 God has spoken in His [1a]holiness:

לַמְנַצֵּחַ עַל־שׁוּשַׁן Psa. 60:1
עֵדוּת מִכְתָּם לְדָוִד לְלַמֵּד ׃

בְּהַצּוֹתוֹ ׀ אֶת אֲרַם Psa. 60:2
נַהֲרַיִם וְאֶת־אֲרַם צוֹבָה וַיָּשָׁב
יוֹאָב וַיַּךְ אֶת־אֱדוֹם בְּגֵיא־
מֶלַח שְׁנֵים עָשָׂר אָלֶף ׃ [3]
אֱלֹהִים זְנַחְתָּנוּ פְרַצְתָּנוּ אָנַפְתָּ
תְּשׁוֹבֵב לָנוּ ׃ [4] הִרְעַשְׁתָּה אֶרֶץ
פְּצַמְתָּהּ רְפָה שְׁבָרֶיהָ כִי־
מָטָה ׃ [5] הִרְאִיתָה עַמְּךָ קָשָׁה
הִשְׁקִיתָנוּ יַיִן תַּרְעֵלָה ׃ [6] נָתַתָּה
לִּירֵאֶיךָ נֵּס לְהִתְנוֹסֵס מִפְּנֵי
קֹשֶׁט סֶלָה ׃ [7] לְמַעַן יֵחָלְצוּן
יְדִידֶיךָ הוֹשִׁיעָה יְמִינְךָ וַעֲנֵנוּ
[וַ][עֲנֵנִי ׃] [8] אֱלֹהִים ׀ דִּבֶּר
בְּקָדְשׁוֹ אֶעְלֹזָה אֲחַלְּקָה שְׁכֶם
וְעֵמֶק סֻכּוֹת אֲמַדֵּד ׃ [9] לִי
גִלְעָד ׀ וְלִי מְנַשֶּׁה וְאֶפְרַיִם
מָעוֹז רֹאשִׁי יְהוּדָה מְחֹקְקִי ׃ [10]
מוֹאָב ׀ סִיר רַחְצִי עַל־אֱדוֹם
אַשְׁלִיךְ נַעֲלִי עָלַי פְּלֶשֶׁת

"I will exult, I will portion out [b]Shechem and measure out the valley of [c]Succoth.

7 "[a]Gilead is Mine, and Manasseh is Mine;

[b]Ephraim also is the [1]helmet of My head;

Judah is My [2c]scepter.

8 "[a]Moab is My washbowl;

Over [b]Edom I shall throw My shoe;

Shout loud, O [c]Philistia, because of Me!"

Psa. 60:9 Who will bring me into the besieged city?

Who [1]will lead me to Edom?

10 Have not You Yourself, O God, [a]rejected us?

And [b]will You not go forth with our armies, O God?

11 O give us help against the adversary,

For [a]deliverance [1]by man is in vain.

12 [1]Through God we shall [a]do valiantly,

And it is He who will [b]tread down our adversaries.

הִתְרָעָעִי : 11 מִי יֹבִלֵנִי עִיר מָצוֹר מִי נָחַנִי עַד־אֱדוֹם : 12 הֲלֹא־אַתָּה אֱלֹהִים זְנַחְתָּנוּ וְלֹא־תֵצֵא אֱלֹהִים בְּצִבְאוֹתֵינוּ : 13 הָבָה־לָּנוּ עֶזְרָת מִצָּר וְשָׁוְא תְּשׁוּעַת אָדָם : 14 בֵּאלֹהִים נַעֲשֶׂה־חָיִל וְהוּא יָבוּס צָרֵינוּ :

References

Psalm 60:0
†Lit *The lily of testimony*
°Possibly, *Epigrammatic Poem* or *Atonement Psalm*
^2 Sam 8:3, 13; 1 Chr 18:3, 12

Psalm 60:1
[1]Or *broken out upon us*
[a]Ps 44:9
[b]2 Sam 5:20
[c]Ps 79:5
[d]Ps 80:3

Psalm 60:2
[1]Or *earth*
[a]Ps 18:7
[b]2 Chr 7:14; Is 30:26

Psalm 60:3
[1]Lit *caused Your people to see*
[2]Lit *wine of staggering*
[a]Ps 66:12; 71:20
[b]Ps 75:8; Is 51:17, 22; Jer 25:15

Psalm 60:4
[1]*Selah* may mean: *Pause, Crescendo* or *Musical interlude*
[a]Ps 20:5; Is 5:26; 11:12; 13:2

Psalm 60:5
[1]Some authorities read *me*
[a]Ps 60:5-12; 108:6-13
[b]Deut 33:12; Ps 127:2; Is 5:1; Jer 11:15
[c]Ps 17:7

Psalm 60:6
[1]Or *sanctuary*
[a]Ps 89:35
[b]Gen 12:6; 33:18; Josh 17:7
[c]Gen 33:17; Josh 13:27

Psalm 60:7
[1]Lit *protection*
[2]Or *lawgiver*
[a]Josh 13:31
[b]Deut 33:17
[c]Gen 49:10

Psalm 60:8
[a]2 Sam 8:2
[b]2 Sam 8:14
[c]2 Sam 8:1

Psalm 60:9
[1]Or *has led*

Psalm 60:10
[a]Ps 60:1; 108:11
[b]Josh 7:12; Ps 44:9

Psalm 60:11
[1]Lit *of*
[a]Ps 146:3

Psalm 60:12
[1]Or *In* or *With*
[a]Num 24:18; Ps 118:16
[b]Ps 44:5; Is 63:3

Targum

Psa. 60:1 For praise. Concerning the ancient testimony between Jacob and Laban. A copy made by David, for instruction.

Psa. 60:2 When David had gathered troops and passed by the Heap of Witness and fought with Aram-on-the-euphrates and Aram Zobah, and afterwards Joab returned and smote the Edomites in the Plain of Salt, and twelve thousand from the army of David and Joab fell. [3] David said, "O God, you have abandoned us, you have attacked us in fierce anger; return to us in your glory." [4] You shook the land of Israel, you made it quake and you flayed it; heal its wounds, for it has become unsteady. [5] You made your people see hardship, you made us drink the wine of execration. [6] You have given those who fear you a sign to be lifted up by, because of the honesty of Abraham forever. [7] Because of the merit of Isaac, those who love you will be delivered; redeem with your right hand because of the piety of Jacob, and accept my prayer. [8] God speaks in his sanctuary: I will be glad, for those of the house of Israel will prevail; I will divide the spoil with the sons of Joseph who dwell in Shechem, and in the plain of Succoth I will measure the measure and divide the booty. [9] My people were of the house of Gilead, and my people were of the house of Manasseh; and the warriors of the house of Ephraim are the strength of my head, and those of the house of Judah are the scribes of my school. [10] I trampled on the Moabites, my feet were dipped in the blood of their warriors as in my washing-basin; on the nape of the neck of the warriors of Edom I set my shoe; shout over the Philistines, O congregation of Israel. [11] Who is he that led me to the ruined city of Tyre? Who is he that guided me to Edom? [12] Is it not you, O LORD? You have abandoned us; and you will not go out, O God, with our forces. [13] Give us help against the oppressor, for in vain is the redemption of a son of man. [14] By the word of the LORD we will exercise might, and he will subdue our oppressors.

Spiritual Awareness

The spiritual rewrite for the verses is in bold.

Introduction

David had an inspired vision of a universal order of nations united in complete harmony. Monotheism had the view of a world working together and universal peace. Paganism's worldview was one of chaos as each god fought with one another on Earth. When David waged war, he tried to conquer nations to join the monotheistic view of one world order.

Superscript

עַל־שׁוּשַׁן עֵדוּת (al shooshan adot) means "upon the rose of the testimony." The pre-Davidic era was a difficult time for Israel. Israel underwent the most severe suffering tests, picturing the people as a thorny rose. The thorny rose availed itself to the thorny protection of the LORD's sovereignty to ward off any brazen attack. In the Song of Songs 2:2, Israel is called a "rose among the thorns." A rose stands surrounded by thorns. The rose will be hurt by the storm's wind no matter its direction. The rose can only protect itself by standing straight and upright. The attacks Israel suffered came from every direction. She must suffer through them and from them all, and it can preserve itself in life only if it remains standing firm and upright while looking up to the LORD on high. Most English versions of this Psalm translate the superscript as "For the choir director, according to Shushan Eduth…" The translation does not consider the calling to the Sefirah Netzach or the value of the Rose of Testimony.

The Targum adds the words "the ancient testimony between Jacob and Laban." The NASB adds, "..when he struggled with Aram-narariam and Arama-zobah, and Joab returned and smote twelve thousand of Edom in the Valley of Salt.

To the Sefirah Netzach Who grants victory, upon the rose of the testimony, an instructional tenet by David.

This verse is added to the superscript in the NASB translation. The Hebrew version includes references to Aram-narariam. The Targum reads as follows.

Psa. 60:2 When David had gathered troops and passed by the Heap of Witness and fought with Aram-on-the-euphrates and Aram Zobah, and afterwards Joab returned and smote the Edomites in the Plain of Salt, and twelve thousand from the army of David and Joab fell.

Aram-narariam (Aram on the Euphrates) implies the territory between the Tigris and Euphrates rivers. Aram Zobah was the capital city of Armenia. Joab was one of David's generals. The Valley of Salt was a part of Edom. Therefore, the territory of David's conquests was from Edom in the south to the Euphrates River in the north.

When he besieged Aram Nataraim and Aram Tzova, Joab returned and smote twelve thousand men of Edom in the valley of salt.

Verse one

David said the LORD had a friendly relationship with Israel and abandoned her because of a change in sentiment or attitude.

O God, You had forsaken us; you made us defenseless; You have been angry, and desired our return.

Verse two

This verse is a reference to the time of the Judges. The twelve tribes acted independently. Different nations were able to attack Israel because they were not together. It was a time for the tribes to realize they needed each other. David wanted the LORD's help to get the tribes to recognize that it was imperative to come together as a powerful nation.

You have made the land shake; you have cleft it; heal its breaches for it totters.

Verse three

The hardship the people suffered was before David's reign. David brought the tribes together for mutual protection and expansion.

You have made Your people see hardship and have made us drink bewilderment like wine.

Verse four

The verses preceding verse four spoke about the painful experiences that Israel had to undergo during the days before the advent of David. This Psalm shows that David thought highly of himself. He saw himself as the savior of Israel. He did build a vast empire of Israel. When the wars ended, Israel was prosperous. The banner can be a metaphor for David.

But you have given a banner to them that revere You, to raise themselves to its height before that might of truth. Meditate on this verse.

Verse five

When Israel suffered in the days of darkness, the LORD always reminded the people that a better day of everlasting freedom was on its way.

Therefore now free those whom You have found worthy of Your love; let Your right-hand show itself only in [works of] salvation and answer me.

Verses six and seven

The LORD showed that better days were ahead because of Israel's victory over Edom.

God has already spoken in His Sanctuary that I should come to great exultation, that I would divide Shechem, that I would apportion the valley of Sukkos.

Gilad shall be mine. Menashe mine, Efrayim the support of my head, Yehudah the pen of my Law.

Verse eight

David expresses his confidence that the LORD will make him victorious over his enemies.

Moab shall be my wash-pot, upon Edom shall I cast my shoe; now let Philistia dare triumph over me!

Verses nine to twelve

The psalmist sees proof that the LORD is again willing to lend His aid to David's military undertakings, giving Israel a future of security and prosperity.

Who will bring me into the besieged city? Who will lead me to Edom?

Have not You Yourself, O God, rejected us? And will You not go forth with our armies, O God?

O give us help against the adversary, for deliverance by man is in vain.

Through God we shall do valiantly, and it is He who will tread down our adversaries.

Complete Psalm Rewrite Emphasizing Spiritual Awareness

To the Sefirah Netzach Who grants victory, upon the rose of the testimony, an instructional tenet by David.

When he besieged Aram Nataraim and Aram Tzova, Joab returned and smote twelve thousand men of Edom in the valley of salt.

O God, You had forsaken us; you made us defenseless; You have been angry, and desired our return.

You have made the land shake; you have cleft it; heal its breaches for it totters.

You have made Your people see hardship and have made us drink bewilderment like wine.

But you have given a banner to them that revere You, to raise themselves to its height before that might of truth. Meditate on this verse.

Therefore now free those whom You have found worthy of Your love; let Your right-hand show itself only in [works of] salvation and answer me.

God has already spoken in His Sanctuary that I should come to great exultation, that I would divide Shechem, that I would apportion the valley of Sukkos.

Gilad shall be mine. Menashe mine, Efrayim the support of my head, Yehudah the pen of my Law.

Moab shall be my wash-pot, upon Edom shall I cast my shoe; now let Philistia dare triumph over me!

Who will bring me into the besieged city? Who will lead me to Edom?

Have not You Yourself, O God, rejected us? And will You not go forth with our armies, O God?

O give us help against the adversary, for deliverance by man is in vain.

Through God we shall do valiantly, and it is He who will tread down our adversaries.

APPENDIX

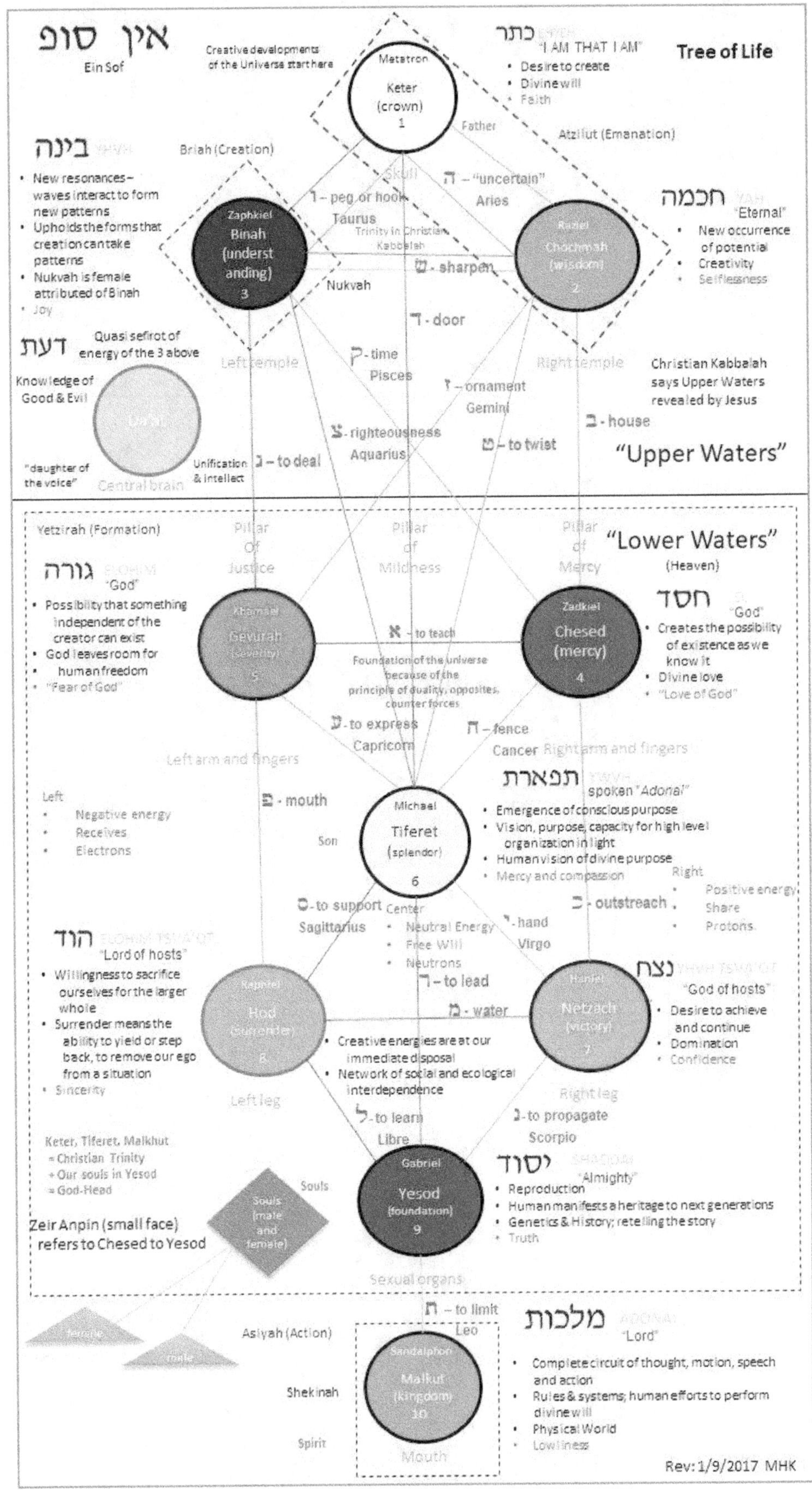
אין סוף
Ein Sof
Creative developments of the Universe start here
כתר
"I AM THAT I AM"
• Desire to create
• Divine will
• Faith
Tree of Life
Metatron
Keter (crown) 1
Father
Atzilut (Emanation)
בינה
• New resonances – waves interact to form new patterns
• Upholds the forms that creation can take patterns
• Nukvah is female attributed of Binah
• Joy
Briah (Creation)
Skull
ה – "uncertain"
Aries
ו – peg or hook
Taurus
Trinity in Christian Kabbalah
חכמה
"Eternal"
• New occurrence of potential
• Creativity
• Selflessness
Zaphkiel
Binah (understanding) 3
Raziel
Chochmah (wisdom) 2
ש – sharpen
Nukvah
ד – door
דעת
Quasi sefirot of energy of the 3 above
Knowledge of Good & Evil
Left temple
Right temple
Christian Kabbalah says Upper Waters revealed by Jesus
ק – time
Pisces
ז – ornament
Gemini
ב – house
"daughter of the voice"
Central brain
Unification & intellect
ג – to deal
צ – righteousness
Aquarius
ט – to twist
"Upper Waters"
Yetzirah (Formation)
Pillar Of Justice
Pillar of Mildness
Pillar of Mercy
"Lower Waters"
(Heaven)
גורה
"God"
• Possibility that something independent of the creator can exist
• God leaves room for human freedom
• "Fear of God"
א – to teach
Foundation of the universe because of the principle of duality, opposites, counter forces
חסד
"God"
• Creates the possibility of existence as we know it
• Divine love
• "Love of God"
Khamael
Gevurah (severity) 5
Zadkiel
Chesed (mercy) 4
Left arm and fingers
ע – to express
Capricorn
ח – fence
Cancer
Right arm and fingers
Left
• Negative energy
• Receives
• Electrons
פ – mouth
תפארת
spoken "Adonai"
• Emergence of conscious purpose
• Vision, purpose, capacity for high level organization in light
• Human vision of divine purpose
• Mercy and compassion
Michael
Tiferet (splendor) 6
Son
Right
Positive energy
Share
Protons
ב – outstreach
ס – to support
Sagittarius
Center
• Neutral Energy
• Free Will
• Neutrons
י – hand
Virgo
הוד
"Lord of hosts"
• Willingness to sacrifice ourselves for the larger whole
• Surrender means the ability to yield or step back, to remove our ego from a situation
• Sincerity
ל – to lead
מ – water
נצח
"God of hosts"
• Desire to achieve and continue
• Domination
• Confidence
Raphael
Hod (surrender) 8
Haniel
Netzach (victory) 7
• Creative energies are at our immediate disposal
• Network of social and ecological interdependence
Left leg
Right leg
Keter, Tiferet, Malkhut = Christian Trinity + Our souls in Yesod = God-Head
Zeir Anpin (small face) refers to Chesed to Yesod
ל – to learn
Libre
Souls (male and female)
Souls
Gabriel
Yesod (foundation) 9
נ – to propagate
Scorpio
יסוד
"Almighty"
• Reproduction
• Human manifests a heritage to next generations
• Genetics & History; retelling the story
• Truth
Sexual organs
ת – to limit
Leo
מלכות
"Lord"
female
male
Asiyah (Action)
Shekinah
Spirit
Sandalphon
Malkut (kingdom) 10
Mouth
• Complete circuit of thought, motion, speech and action
• Rules & systems; human efforts to perform divine will
• Physical World
• Lowliness
Rev: 1/9/2017 MHK

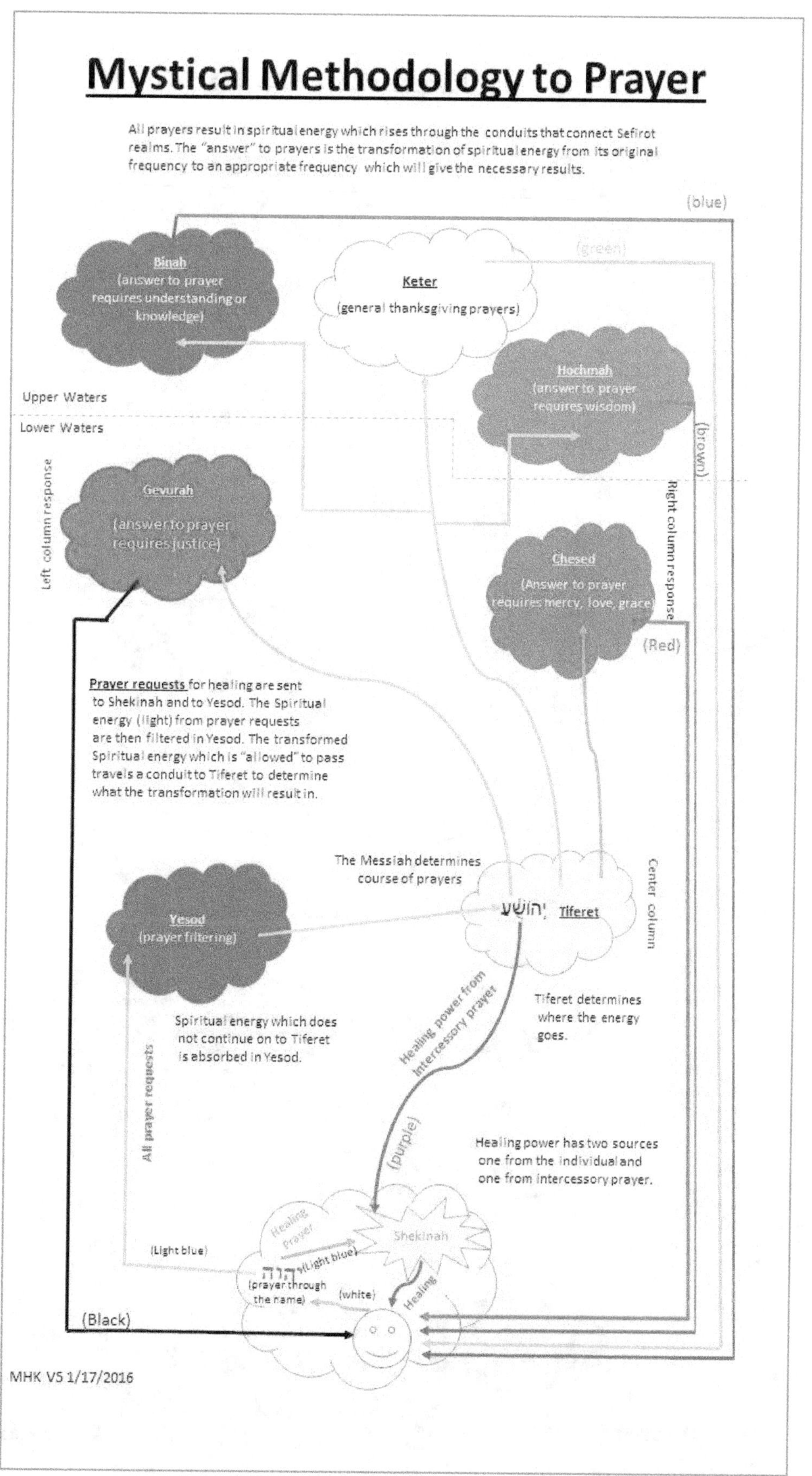

Mystical Methodology to Prayer
All prayers result in spiritual energy which rises through the conduits that connect Sefirot realms. The "answer" to prayers is the transformation of spiritual energy from its original frequency to an appropriate frequency which will give the necessary results.
(blue)
(green)
Binah
(answer to prayer requires understanding or knowledge)
Keter
(general thanksgiving prayers)
Hochmah
(answer to prayer requires wisdom)
Upper Waters
Lower Waters
(brown)
Left column response
Gevurah
(answer to prayer requires justice)
Chesed
(Answer to prayer requires mercy, love, grace)
Right column response
(Red)
Prayer requests for healing are sent to Shekinah and to Yesod. The Spiritual energy (light) from prayer requests are then filtered in Yesod. The transformed Spiritual energy which is "allowed" to pass travels a conduit to Tiferet to determine what the transformation will result in.
The Messiah determines course of prayers
יהושע Tiferet
Center column
Yesod
(prayer filtering)
Tiferet determines where the energy goes.
Spiritual energy which does not continue on to Tiferet is absorbed in Yesod.
All prayer requests
Healing power from Intercessory prayer
(purple)
Healing power has two sources one from the individual and one from intercessory prayer.
Healing Prayer
(Light blue)
Shekinah
(Light blue)
יהוה
(prayer through the name)
(white)
Healing
(Light blue)
(Black)
MHK V5 1/17/2016

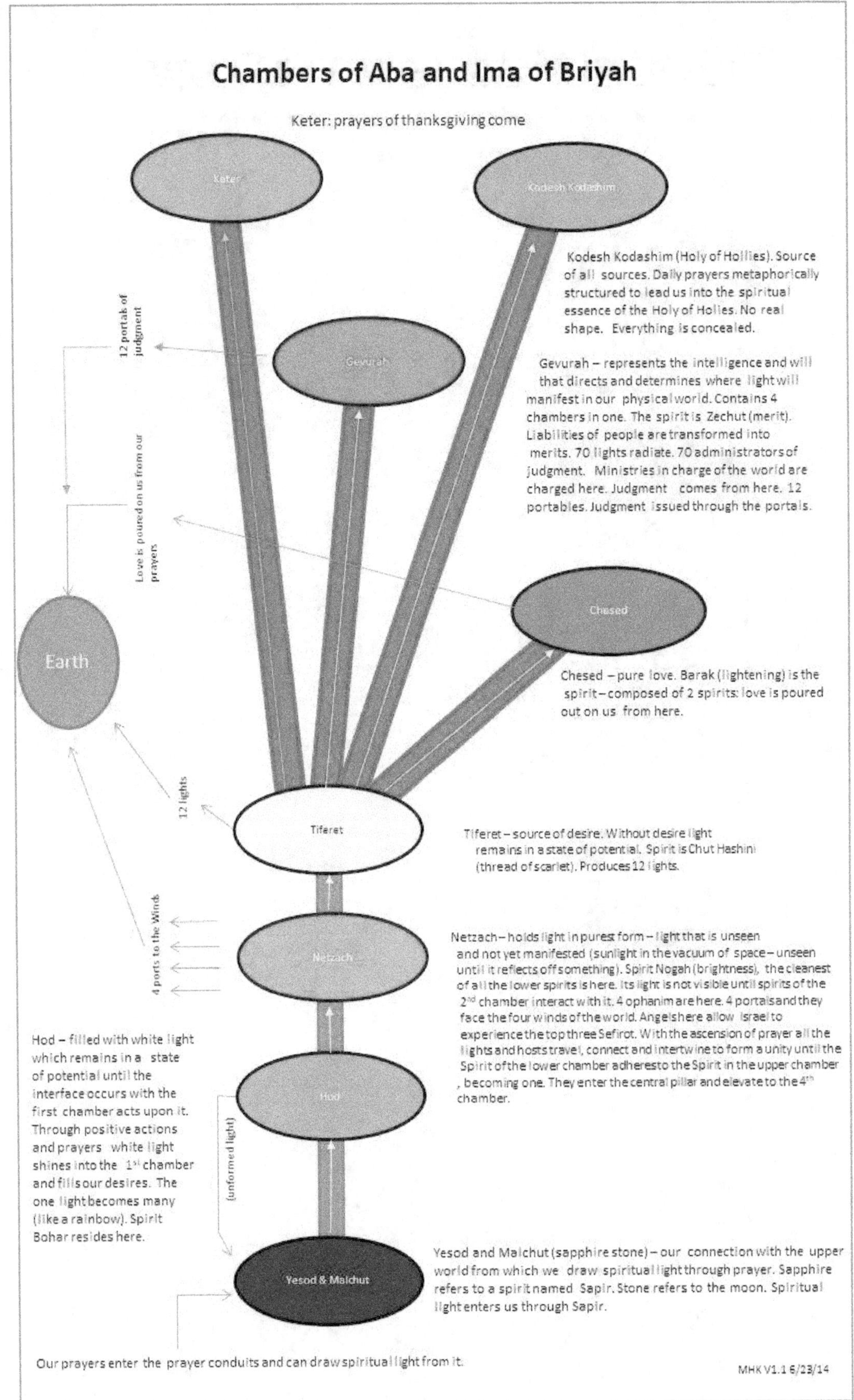

Chambers of Aba and Ima of Briyah
Keter: prayers of thanksgiving come
Keter
Kodesh Kodashim
Gevurah
Chesed
Earth
Tiferet
Netzach
Hod
Yesod & Malchut
12 portals of judgment
Love is poured on us from our prayers
12 lights
4 ports to the Winds
(unformed light)
Kodesh Kodashim (Holy of Hollies). Source of all sources. Daily prayers metaphorically structured to lead us into the spiritual essence of the Holy of Hollies. No real shape. Everything is concealed.
Gevurah – represents the intelligence and will that directs and determines where light will manifest in our physical world. Contains 4 chambers in one. The spirit is Zechut (merit). Liabilities of people are transformed into merits. 70 lights radiate. 70 administrators of judgment. Ministries in charge of the world are charged here. Judgment comes from here. 12 portables. Judgment issued through the portals.
Chesed – pure love. Barak (lightening) is the spirit – composed of 2 spirits: love is poured out on us from here.
Tiferet – source of desire. Without desire light remains in a state of potential. Spirit is Chut Hashini (thread of scarlet). Produces 12 lights.
Netzach – holds light in purest form – light that is unseen and not yet manifested (sunlight in the vacuum of space – unseen until it reflects off something). Spirit Nogah (brightness), the cleanest of all the lower spirits is here. Its light is not visible until spirits of the 2nd chamber interact with it. 4 ophanim are here. 4 portals and they face the four winds of the world. Angels here allow Israel to experience the top three Sefirot. With the ascension of prayer all the lights and hosts travel, connect and intertwine to form a unity until the Spirit of the lower chamber adheres to the Spirit in the upper chamber, becoming one. They enter the central pillar and elevate to the 4th chamber.
Hod – filled with white light which remains in a state of potential until the interface occurs with the first chamber acts upon it. Through positive actions and prayers white light shines into the 1st chamber and fills our desires. The one light becomes many (like a rainbow). Spirit Bohar resides here.
Yesod and Malchut (sapphire stone) – our connection with the upper world from which we draw spiritual light through prayer. Sapphire refers to a spirit named Sapir. Stone refers to the moon. Spiritual light enters us through Sapir.
Our prayers enter the prayer conduits and can draw spiritual light from it.
MHK V1.1 6/23/14

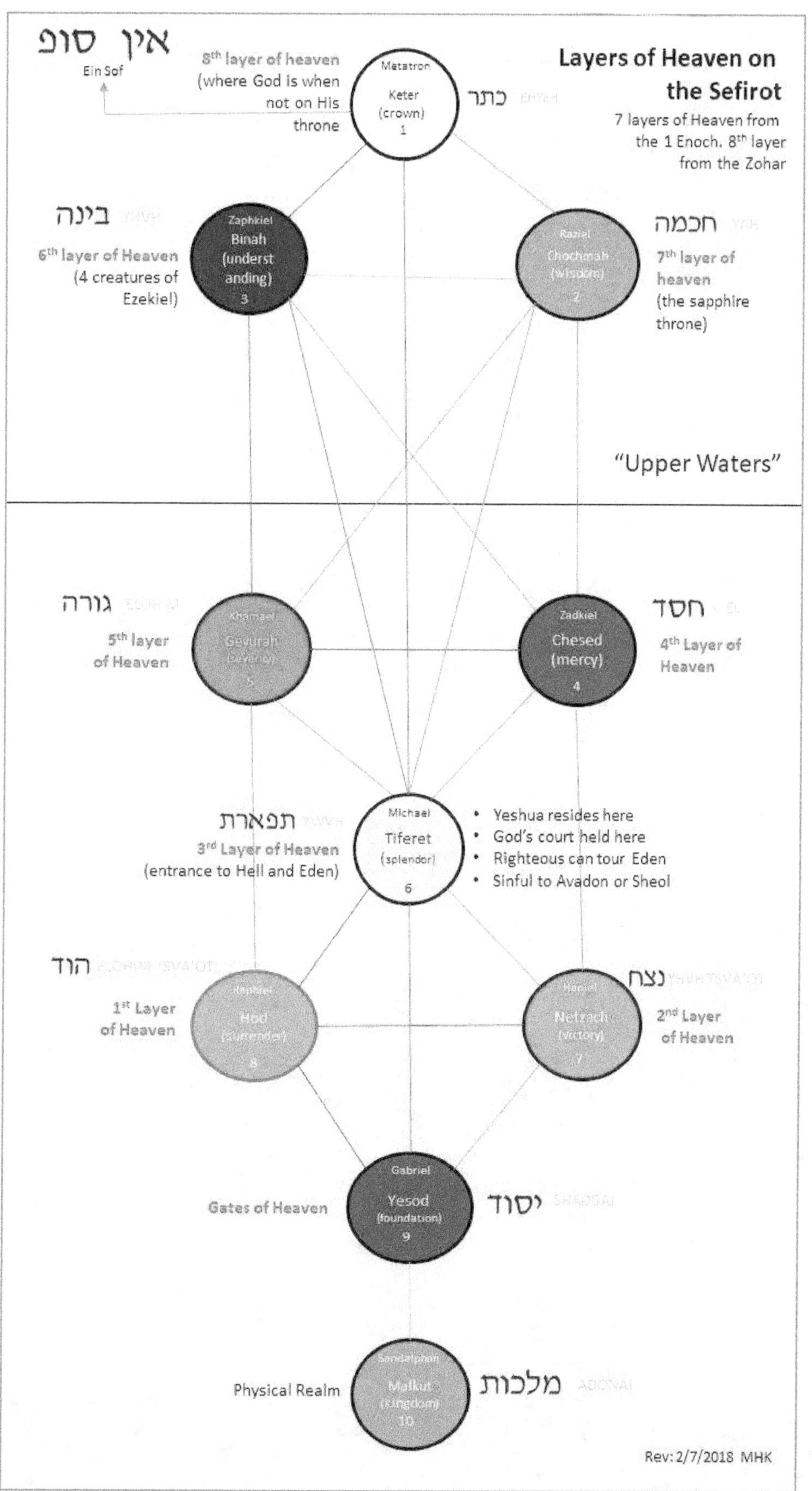
אין סוף
Ein Sof

8th layer of heaven (where God is when not on His throne)

Layers of Heaven on the Sefirot
7 layers of Heaven from the 1 Enoch. 8th layer from the Zohar

Metatron
Keter (crown)
1
כתר

בינה
6th layer of Heaven (4 creatures of Ezekiel)

Zaphkiel
Binah (understanding)
3

Raziel
Chochmah (wisdom)
2

חכמה
7th layer of heaven (the sapphire throne)

"Upper Waters"

גבורה
5th layer of Heaven

Khamael
Gevurah (severity)
5

Zadkiel
Chesed (mercy)
4

חסד
4th Layer of Heaven

תפארת
3rd Layer of Heaven (entrance to Hell and Eden)

Michael
Tiferet (splendor)
6

• Yeshua resides here
• God's court held here
• Righteous can tour Eden
• Sinful to Avadon or Sheol

הוד
1st Layer of Heaven

Raphael
Hod (surrender)
8

Haniel
Netzach (victory)
7

נצח
2nd Layer of Heaven

Gabriel
Yesod (foundation)
9

Gates of Heaven

יסוד

Physical Realm

Sandalphon
Malkut (kingdom)
10

מלכות

Rev: 2/7/2018 MHK